The Diversity Principle

Friend or Foe of the First Amendment?

THE DIVERSITY PRINCIPLE

FRIEND OR FOE OF THE First Amendment?

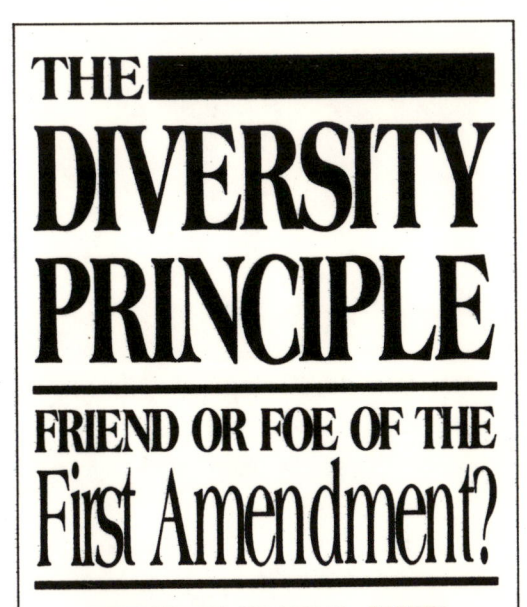

EDITED BY CRAIG R. SMITH

WITH A PREFACE BY SENATOR ROBERT KASTEN

Published by
the media institute
Washington, D.C.

The Diversity Principle: Friend or Foe of the First Amendment?

Copyright ©1989 The Media Institute

All rights reserved. No part of this publication may be reproduced or transmitted in any form without permission in writing from the publisher.

First printing October 1989.

Published by The Media Institute, Washington, D.C.

Printed in the United States of America.

ISBN: 0-937790-40-0

Library of Congress Catalog Card Number: 89-63287

Table of Contents

Acknowledgment — vii

Preface — ix
Senator Robert Kasten (R-Wisconsin)

I. The Evolution of the Diversity Principle — 1

II. The Misapplication of the Diversity Principle to Broadcast Media — 9

III. The Misapplication of the Diversity Principle to Cable Television — 25

IV. The Misapplication of the Diversity Principle to the Telecommunications Industry — 37

V. Conclusion — 47

Notes — 55

Acknowledgment

The Media Institute expresses its profound thanks to Richard A. Hindman with the firm of Wilkinson, Barker, Knauer & Quinn for his significant contribution to the research and writing of Chapters 3 and 4. The Editor, Craig Smith, researched and wrote the other chapters and edited the entire manuscript.

Preface

Over the last eight years, many of us in Congress have worked hard to free Americans from the fetters of unnecessary government regulation. In no area has that effort been more important than in the marketplace of ideas. The free flow of information ensures that our citizens are fully informed about the issues of the day; it ensures that consumers understand the merits of the products and services they purchase; and it ensures that misrepresentation can be uncovered in the give and take of full and robust debate.

While we have many important freedoms, freedom of expression may be the most important because it supports all our other liberties. Justice Benjamin Cardozo expressed this notion well in 1937, when he wrote, "freedom of thought, and speech . . . [is] the indispensible condition, of nearly every other form of freedom." Perhaps that is why the Founders wrote categorical and explicit language defending freedom of speech and press into the Bill of Rights. The case law that has developed since the ratification of the First Amendment in 1791 gives government the power to curtail dangerous, subversive, prurient, obscene, and libelous speech. At the same time, the courts have made clear that we must not restrict sources of valuable information. The courts have attempted to make a diversity of opinion and information available to all.

In the monograph that follows, the Freedom of Expression Foundation and The Media Institute examine the ways in which some in our system have misapplied the "diversity principle," and how this misapplication has choked the stream of information that flows into the marketplace of ideas. In some cases, as with the so-called "fairness doctrine," well-intentioned content regulations have actually had a chilling effect on free speech. In other cases—regulation of the communications industry comes to mind—structural limitations have slowed the development of new technology and eliminated major providers of information.

The Freedom of Expression Foundation and The Media Institute have battled in the courts, government agencies, and Congress to advance First Amendment freedoms. The Foundation led the fight to repeal the fairness doctrine; the Institute has entered several prominent cases to try to secure the First Amendment rights of the cable industry. Together they are working to remove many restrictions imposed on information providers. That is why they are uniquely qualified to assess the current regulatory scheme, and to suggest reforms.

To my knowledge, this is the first study to integrate successfully our historic First Amendment rights, recent court rulings, and free-market principles. This study will bring those of us who make the laws, and those who rule on their constitutionality, to a deeper and fuller understanding of how we can apply First Amendment protections in an information age.

The study includes a description of measures which merit serious attention by all policymakers in this area. As we celebrate the Bicentennial of the ratification of our Constitution, we must continue to protect the free and open marketplace of ideas first proposed by the Founders of this nation.

Senator Robert Kasten
Washington, D.C.
September 1989

I. The Evolution of the Diversity Principle

The original goal of freedom of expression and assembly protected by the First Amendment was to protect the right of everyone to participate in the marketplace of ideas—not to promote diversity in that marketplace. However, today some people would actually place the need for diversity mechanisms above the sanctity of the marketplace itself. To enlighten and help correct this situation, this study begins with a look at the evolution of the so-called "diversity principle" and then proceeds to examine its misapplication to various media.

The United States was the first country to write into its Constitution a guarantee of freedom of speech and press. The reasons for this historic amendment enlighten the intent of the Founders and the proper application of the amendment today. In the Old World, the printing press was strictly controlled by ruling monarchs and the church. Censorship was common. In England, from which we derived much of our common-law understanding of communications issues, the printing press was restricted from the time of Henry VII (1485-1509) and was licensed from the time of Henry VIII (1509-1547); the doctrine of seditious libel was often used to punish editors and publishers. In fact, the Tudor monarchs, particularly Elizabeth I, were adept at using the licensing process to curry favor with the press or force it to support their programs. By the time the Puritans left England for America in 1630, there were only 55 presses in England: 53 in London under the King's nose and one each at Oxford and Cambridge, where ecclesiastical authorities monitored what was published. Worse still, the 55 presses were under the control of only 23 master printers, all of whom were given monopoly rights over what they printed.

Three thousand miles from England, the printing press in America was freer and more provocative, particularly in the hands of Benjamin Franklin, Thomas Payne, and Samuel Adams. By the time of the Stamp Act Crisis of 1765, editors and publishers had developed an intricate network for the distribution of news. When Patrick Henry delivered his famous speech attacking the Stamp Act, it was reprinted throughout the colonies, giving heart to those as far away as Massachusetts. When British troops "massacred" civilians in Boston in 1770, the citizens of Charleston, South Carolina, knew about it a few weeks later.

Thus, when the colonies declared their independence from England, many wrote new constitutions guaranteeing freedom of speech and the press. George Mason in Virginia, for example, wrote that "Freedom of the press is the bulwark of liberty." The Pennsylvania "Frame" of 1776 protected free speech and free press.

When a new Constitution was submitted to the states in 1787 for ratification, its major failing was an absence of a bill of rights. That situation was remedied by 1791 with the passage of ten amendments to the Constitution. The first of these said that "Congress shall make no law . . . abridging the freedom of speech or of the press." The Supreme Court's interpretation of this amendment has guaranteed that the government may not impose content controls on the press, and that those who seek judgments against the press must meet a very high standard of proof before the press can be penalized. Perhaps the best rationale for this position was given in 1964 in *New York Times v. Sullivan*[1] when the Court said that debate "on public issues should be uninhibited, robust and wide open . . . ."

Earlier, the Court had given another rationale for what would become the diversity principle. In *Associated Press v. United States*,[2] which was decided in 1945, the Supreme Court said that "an underlying goal of the First Amendment is to achieve the widest possible dissemination of information from diverse and antagonistic sources." Taken together, these two decisions reinforce the Founders' belief that an informed electorate is the key to a thriving democracy. An open, active, and diverse marketplace of ideas is the best way to disseminate information to the public and assure that citizens are educated enough to carry out their responsibilities. This open and free flow of information prevents government interference and encourages diversity.

In 1969, in *Red Lion Broadcasting Co. v. FCC*,[3] the Supreme Court tried an experiment by building on its decision in the *NBC* case of 1943. It turned away from the marketplace model and condoned government-induced diversity for the electronic media:

> Because of the scarcity of radio frequencies, the Government is permitted to put restraints on licensees in favor of others whose views should be expressed on this unique medium . . . . It is the right of the viewers and listeners, not the right of the broadcasters which is paramount. It is the purpose of the First Amendment to preserve an uninhibited marketplace of ideas in which truth will ultimately prevail, rather than to countenance monopolization of that market, whether it be by the government itself or a private licensee.

This controversial decision is discussed in greater detail in the next chapter; however, we note here that it was the first time the Court determined that the content of a communication medium could be regulated to assure access to a diversity of opinion. Such a dangerous and risky power was vested in the government because the medium was considered scarce and therefore unavailable to all who sought to use it.[4] In short, because the Court believed broadcast signals to be a scarce medium, it said that broadcast licensees did not qualify for the kind of freedom afforded to the print media. It reaffirmed print's sacrosanct status unanimously in 1974 in *Miami Herald Publishing Co. v. Tornillo*;[5] the Court declared an equal-space statute *inapplicable* to the only major newspaper in Miami, a far scarcer resource than a broadcasting signal.

The *Red Lion* decision, which the Court has indicated a willingness to reconsider,[6] allowed the Federal Communications Commission (FCC) to impose content controls not only on radio and television, but on cable. In issuing the order, the FCC said that the content rules, which included editorial policy,

> would be grossly circumvented if the CATV subscriber receives both sides when he tunes his television set to a broadcast channel at a time when broadcast program material is being presented but only one side when he switches to a CATV origination channel or stays tuned to the broadcast channel at a time when CATV origination has been substituted for deleted broadcast material.[7]

The FCC, employing a station-by-station diversity rule, forced cable operators to present balanced programming on each origination channel instead of on the system as a whole. This rule was implemented even though every non-origination channel that the system carried was already subject to the fairness doctrine at its point of original broadcast. Here was a classic case of regulation by association. Said the Commission, "Since CATV systems use broadcast signals as the backbone of the service they provide, they come within the regulation of this agency, if reasonably related to the public interest."[8] Eventually, the FCC went on to claim that it had the right to impose the fairness doctrine, the personal attack rule, and the political editorial rule on new broadcast technologies such as teletext.[9] As we shall see in the chapters that follow, it can be argued that no other government agency has so widely imposed a regulation meant to affect only one medium of communication. The rationale for this imposition has consistently been that diversity must exist on a station-by-station basis for the First Amendment to be served. This approach may be likened to enforcing a diversity rule on each columnist of a newspaper.

While imposing this content rule on cable to assure diversity, the FCC also applied a structural rule to the same end. In 1970, the FCC limited cross-ownership between telephone and cable companies.[10] The Congress and courts in a series of laws and decisions held that, because telephone companies owned poles and lines, they would compete unfairly with rival cable companies. When the Bell Operating Companies (BOCs) were created from the divestiture of AT&T, approved by the court in 1982, they were expressly prevented from providing cable services.[11] Thus, one economically viable entity which could provide competing cable offerings to consumers is prevented from doing so.

The cable industry is also besieged by local governments which, in return for franchise rights, have imposed all manner of content controls on systems. The Cable Communications Policy Act of 1984 was designed to relieve some instances of local interference in programming content. Furthermore, courts have generally equated cable rights with newspaper rights. In *Home Box Office, Inc. v. FCC*,[12] for example, the Supreme Court said in 1977:

> [S]carcity which is the result solely of economic conditions is apparently insufficient to justify even limited government intrusion into the First Amendment rights of the conventional press, and there is nothing in the record before us to suggest a constitutional distinction between cable television and newspapers on this point.

But egregious cases remain. Periodically, a court decision is announced that grants localities the right to interfere with a cable system's operation on the ground that the cable system deserves less First Amendment protection than other media. Cities have prevented a second cable system from entering; they have imposed huge tax levies after cable systems have been established; they have demanded not only "local access channels" but guarantees that governmental meetings will be broadcast live. Professor Philip Kurland of the University of Chicago believes these requirements to be unconstitutional:

> The First Amendment should also have made it clear to the politicians that they have no constitutional power to seek the right to communicate through [cable] any more than they could seek the right to communicate by way of the other print and electronic media. The right to speak and to publish is not a saleable commodity, and certainly not one to be bartered by government. What local governments have a right to charge for is the use of public rights of way to string wires. And that can be sold only at prices that bear a reasonable relationship to cost. They cannot inhibit free speech by charging for the right to engage in it. The First Amendment sees to that.[13]

Chapter Three of this study reveals that recent court rulings may be reversing this misapplication of the diversity principle to the benefit of consumers, the cable industry, and the telephone industry. For now, however, restrictions on cable are applied in terms of content, market incentives, and local requirements. This position runs counter to earlier Supreme Court rulings which argued that anything which infringed on the ability of the public to receive information would be antithetical to the Founders' dream.

Lawrence Tribe, in his acclaimed study *American Constitutional Law*, cites three dangers resulting from imposed access laws:

> [T]he danger of deterring those items of coverage that will trigger duties of affording access at the media's expense; the danger of inviting manipulation of the media by whichever bureaucrats are entrusted to assure access; and the danger of escalating from access regulation to much more dubious exercises of governmental control.[14]

In *Miami Herald Publishing Co. v. Tornillo*,[15] the Supreme Court unanimously ruled that regulations enforcing diversity interfered with the editorial process and were a violation of the First Amendment rights of newspapers:

> [E]ach point in the implementation of a remedy such as an enforceable right of access necessarily calls for some mechanism, either governmental or consensual. If it is governmental coercion, this at once brings about a confrontation with the express provisions of the First Amendment and the judicial gloss on that Amendment developed over the years.

The Court returned to that standard as recently as 1988 in *City of Lakewood v. Plain Dealer Publishing Co.*[16] The Court struck down an ordinance of the city of Lakewood, Ohio, which regulated the placement of newspaper vending machines on a scarce resource, namely city sidewalks. Justice William J. Brennan, Jr. wrote the majority opinion which said "the Constitution requires that the city establish neutral criteria to insure that the licensing decision is not based on the content or viewpoint of the speech being considered." This monograph argues that the same position should be taken with regard to electronic media, particularly broadcasting, cablecasting, and information services.

The use of the "diversity principle" for rhetorical ends reached a low point in the AT&T divestiture. Judge Harold Greene used the phrase to argue that phone companies, particularly the seven new regional Bell Operating Companies (BOCs), should be prevented from engaging in electronic publishing. The newspaper publishers were worried that phone companies might provide classified ads and advertising that would take business away from newspapers. In a classic case of overkill, Judge Greene, who presided over the AT&T breakup, sided with the publishers. "[I]n promoting diversity in sources of information, the values underlying the First Amendment coincide with the policy of the antitrust laws."[17] Judge Greene's action was preventive and part of a 1982 consent decree which ended the antitrust suit brought by the Justice Department against AT&T in 1974. But the ruling applied not only to AT&T but to the new companies formed from the divestiture. The divestiture became effective on January 1, 1984, and held the seven BOCs to an agreement they had not made. Furthermore, since the BOCs had never engaged in electronic publishing, no one could know whether they would engage in anticompetitive behavior or that such behavior would diminish diversity. Judge Greene simply assumed that such would be the case and thereby employed the "diversity principle" as a legal tool for antitrust purposes.

In 1987, the Justice Department asked that the restrictions on the BOCs be removed: "The government recommends removal of the decree prohibition on the Bell companies' provision of information services because that prohibition is not necessary to protect competition and *may be depriving large parts of our society of the benefits of the information age.*"[18] The Justice Department, joined by the FCC and the National Telecommunications and Information Administration, went on to argue that true diversity is more likely to occur if telephone companies are free to provide information services because they are the only economically viable providers of some services and the only technologically capable providers of others. In short, said the Justice Department, Judge Greene by his order had stood the diversity principle on its head. He was actually precluding the development of new access, information technologies, and services.

On September 10, 1987, Judge Greene refused to relax content restrictions preventing the BOCs from engaging in information services. He accepted the argument that because the phone companies had a monopoly over the distribution lines to homes and offices, the BOCs should not be permitted to have any interest in the information that is transmitted.[19] In 1990, the case will be reviewed again. Chapter Four of this study addresses the issue in detail, including the question of whether Judge Greene's ruling is retarding commercial development of information services and harming international trade possibilities.

In this introduction, however, our purpose has been to show how the diversity principle evolved and has been misused to support court cases, FCC rules, and laws that are inimical to an open marketplace of ideas. We have come a long way from the Supreme Court's 1975 statement in *Buckley v. Valeo*[20] that "the concept that government may restrict the speech of some elements in our society in order to enhance the relative voice of others is wholly foreign to the First Amendment . . . ." In the chapters that follow, we will examine the implications of the station-by-station imposition of a diversity rule, and its imposition in a way that precludes certain carriers from providing any information at all. We will argue that in an effort to guarantee diversity, even the Supreme Court has on occasion closed certain shops in the free marketplace of ideas. We will also review some recent cases where the Supreme Court appears to have changed its mind. And we will look at cases which will give the Supreme Court opportunity to re-open the marketplace of ideas to all possible participants.

II. The Misapplication of the Diversity Principle to Broadcast Media

Perhaps the best example of the government's confused attitude toward the media is the difference in the way print and electronic media have been regulated. The last serious attempt to regulate the content of a newspaper was swept away by a unanimous Supreme Court in 1974. As we have seen, in *Miami Herald Publishing Co. v. Tornillo* the Court held that equal space provisions written into Florida's law were unconstitutional.[1]

The circumstances of the case are interesting because some believe they justified limits on the First Amendment protection of a newspaper. Pat Tornillo was running for public office in Miami; his opponent was endorsed by the *Miami Herald*. Tornillo invoked a little known law passed in 1913 that required newspapers to give equal space to the opponents of those they endorsed. The *Herald* refused and lost the case unanimously in the Florida Supreme Court, which cited *restrictions that had been placed on the electronic media* as one of its rationales for upholding the imposition of them on the *Herald*. Citing the U.S. Supreme Court's ruling of 1969, *Red Lion Broadcasting Co. v. FCC*[2] (see below), the Florida Court ruled that the *Miami Herald* owed Tornillo equal space because of its endorsement of his opponent.

The Supreme Court never mentioned its *Red Lion* decision when it reversed the Florida Supreme Court and struck down the Florida law. It simply said that freedom of the press was inviolable. Thus, the printed press in America retained strong protection from government interference.

This has not been true with electronic media even when they serve the same purposes as newspapers. The reasons for this double standard can be traced back to the development of radio. As radio became popular, signals began to interfere with one another and with naval operations. Several laws passed between 1911 and 1922 proved ineffective. As a result, in 1927 Congress passed the Dill-White Radio Act which created the Federal Radio Commission (FRC), the forerunner of the Federal Communications Commission (FCC).

In the process of passing this legislation, which required the federal licensing of radio stations, Congress added that the stations had to operate in the "public interest" and had to afford candidates for office an equal opportunity for air time. The first test of the new law came in 1929 when a radio station owned by the Chicago Federation of Labor was not allowed to increase its air time because the Federal Radio Commission deemed its *programming* not to be in the public interest. In 1931 the FRC *denied* a license based on a review of programming content. In 1932, Congress tried to expand the equal opportunities rules to include public referenda on issues, but the effort fell victim to a pocket veto by President Hoover. In 1934, Congress re-wrote the 1927 Act into the Communications Act. The 1934 Act replaced the FRC with the Federal Communications Commission and gave it the power to regulate telephone, telegraph, and television. Government interference with the content of broadcast programming has been the rule ever since.

For example, in May of 1940, the FCC handed down its *Mayflower Broadcasting Corp.* decision in which a licensee (the Yankee Network) was granted a renewal contingent upon its agreement not to editorialize. "The broadcaster cannot be an advocate," the FCC said. This breach of First Amendment rights was justified on the grounds that the broadcaster was beholden to the government for its license, and hence had restricted rights under this arrangement.

In 1943, the National Broadcasting Company (NBC) took the FCC to the Supreme Court to force repeal of the rules governing content. But partially because NBC programmed 86 percent of nighttime broadcasting, the Supreme Court ruled against the network and reinforced the initial rationale for the legislation: that a scarcity of outlets exists for broadcast programming, and therefore the government has a right to license the electromagnetic spectrum and assess its use in terms of programming.[3]

To correct the *Mayflower* rule, in 1949 the FCC promulgated a new rule called the "fairness doctrine." It required coverage of local issues of *importance* and presentation of *contrasting* points of view on those issues,[4] in an attempt to promote a diversity of views in the marketplace of ideas. Despite a stormy legislative history during which attempts were made to codify the doctrine, or at least to claim that it was mandated by statute,[5] the fairness doctrine was a major measure of the performance of broadcast stations until the FCC repealed it in 1987.[6]

The issue of controls over broadcasters came to a head in the *Red Lion* case of 1969. Compare the circumstances of this case to that of *Miami Herald*. Red Lion Broadcasting owned a small radio station, WGCB in Red Lion, Pennsylvania, a town of less than 6,000 persons. Listeners in the small town had access to over 20 other radio stations at the time of this incident (1964). They also had access to cable television, of which about half the households took advantage. There was, in short, no scarcity of informational services in Red Lion. During the election of 1964, WGCB aired a five-minute syndicated editorial by the Reverend Billy James Hargis of the "Christian Crusade." In the editorial, Hargis attacked Fred Cook, a member of the Democratic National Committee. Neither Cook nor Hargis were members of the community of Red Lion, Pennsylvania.

Cook demanded time for a response to Hargis' editorial. WGCB said that Cook would have to pay for his response time; the cost would be $5. Cook refused and the case wound up before the Supreme Court in 1969. The Court ruled in favor of Cook, sticking to the old argument that the electromagnetic spectrum is limited in size. (Later, Fred Friendly discovered that Cook had been working with Democratic Party officials in a campaign to suppress right-wing opinion by means of the "fairness doctrine"; Cook's *Nation* article, the book he wrote about Goldwater, and possibly even his suit against WGCB were products of this effort.)

The "Scarcity Rationale"

Until 1987, electronic media were subject to the fairness doctrine and are still subject to governmental controls over the content of what is broadcast. The *Red Lion* case provides the operant precedent. These controls include a personal attack rule, an equal time provision, and equal access rules.[7] In the first chapter of this monograph, we made clear that the Court approved these controls in the belief that they would ensure "diversity" of opinion over a "scarce" resource. Print media are free from such controls, with the *Miami Herald* case providing the operant precedent. The irony in all of this is that television stations now outnumber daily newspapers and that there are about eight times as many radio stations as either of the other media. Yet television, radio, and even cable programmers have been subject to the fairness doctrine and continue to be subject to other controls because they are deemed to be trustees of a "scarce" resource.

There are many problems with the scarcity rationale, which has been used to justify this misapplication of the diversity principle. First, scarcity was not a concern of the Founders when they drafted and submitted the First Amendment to the states for ratification. Only a handful of newspapers existed at the time. They were expensive to operate and hence a scarce voice. Yet, despite their highly partisan nature, newspapers were protected from government intrusion. Furthermore, given that all the presses in England had been licensed since the time of Henry VIII, it is unlikely that our Founders would have favored a licensing scheme even if they accepted scarcity as a rationale for the imposition of some sort of controls.

Second, "scarcity" is a relative term that provides government with an arbitrary method of controlling the media. Judge Robert Bork understood this well in the *TRAC* case when he wrote:

> It is certainly true that broadcast frequencies are scarce but it is unclear why that fact justifies content regulation of broadcasting in a way that would be intolerable if applied to the editorial process of the print media. All economic goods are scarce, not least the newsprint, ink, delivery trucks, computers, and other resources that go into the production and dissemination of print journalism. Not everyone who wishes to publish a newspaper, or even a pamphlet, may do so. Since scarcity is a universal fact, it can hardly explain regulation in one context and not another ....[8]

The Court went on to suggest that the tension between *Miami Herald* and *Red Lion* might be resolved on the ground that, "while scarcity characterizes both print and broadcast media, the latter must be operating under conditions of greater 'scarcity' than the former. This, however, is unpersuasive. There is nothing uniquely scarce about the broadcast spectrum."[9]

Bork recognized that today's media marketplace is characterized by great abundance and natural diversity. Ninety-six percent of households receive five or more television stations; 71 percent of those households receive nine or more stations. Today there are over 7,000 cable systems in the United States and over half of the nation's households subscribe. Cable is now available to more than two-thirds of American homes and the percentage is growing weekly. Without reviewing the growth of radio, multi-point distribution systems, and satellite relays, it is sufficient to say that the problem is not scarcity of diverse news and opinion—the problem is trying to choose among all of the available outlets.

In the *Miami Herald* case, the Supreme Court considered a newspaper reader sophisticated and intelligent enough to form his or her own opinion. In *Red Lion*, however, the radio listener was treated as one who must be protected by a governmental agency which assures "fairness." What makes this proposition even more suspect is that the newspaper reader and radio listener could be the same person, and the news they receive may very well come from the same source, for example, the AP or UPI wire. Furthermore, the radio listener has a plethora of stations to listen to, along with the option of turning off the broadcast. It is therefore very odd that the scarcity rationale is applied to the electronic media when it is not applied to less diverse print media.

One also hears defenders of enforced diversity argue that scarcity should not be measured in terms of numbers but in terms of price. They claim that the expense of starting a broadcast station precludes most people from access and therefore licenses are a scarce resource which should be controlled by the federal government. This argument confuses the audience with the license. There are many licenses available across the country, but no one wants them because they are not economically viable. What most advocates want is access to a large audience. But these audiences have been built and maintained by the individual broadcaster who has paid a great deal of money for the staff and programming to attract the audience; it did not come with the license. Thus, to argue that the price of purchasing a particular station makes all licenses scarce is disingenuous.

Finally, some favoring content regulations argue that anyone can start a newspaper with a mimeograph machine and gain access to the public. They claim this is not the case with the electronic media and therefore it should be controlled. In fact, anyone *can* broadcast if he can afford a bull horn (they are cheaper than mimeograph machines), and will be more effective given that what is said from a loudspeaker is harder to block than what's handed out on the street and usually tossed into a trash can without a reading. Clearly, comparing newspapers to mimeograph machines raises disingenuousness to new levels.

Such considerations forced Justice William O. Douglas to conclude:

> TV and Radio ... are [ ] included in the concept of press as used in the First Amendment and therefore are entitled to live under the laissez-faire regime which the First Amendment sanctions.[10]

The Burden of Regulation

Abiding by content controls is one condition the government imposes on broadcasters in return for a license. When a station's license comes up for renewal, the government examines the station's files to determine whether the broadcaster has been "operating in the public interest." According to a National Association of Broadcasters (NAB) survey of 40 contested license renewal proceedings, the average case lasted eight years. Radio stations spent an average of $600,000 and television stations $1.2 million in contested cases for legal fees. "Fairness" complaints used to play a large role in such proceedings.

In the three years from 1973 to 1976, over 13,000 "fairness" complaints were filed at the FCC. That is an average of 1.3 per station per three-year period. The number of complaints in the '80s was even higher before repeal of the fairness doctrine. But very few of these cases, *less than* 15 in the time period mentioned, resulted in sanctions. Most of these calls for diversity were groundless.[11] However, they were effective in harassing stations because broadcasters had great difficulty determining which of these many complaints would be taken seriously by the FCC. For example, NBC and one of its local affiliates became embroiled in a fairness complaint concerning their broadcast of the the mini-series "Holocaust." Friedrich Berg filed a complaint arguing that the April 1978 "docu-drama" was "generally anti-German and pro-Jewish." He demanded an opportunity to oppose the "allegation of a German policy of Jewish extermination during World War II." It was a year before the case was dismissed.

Government programming standards have other bad results. They lead to uniform, bland programming; that is, they reduce diversity. A classic case was recently decided and shows how the rules can work.

Simon Geller is a daylight radio broadcaster in Gloucester, Massachusetts. After experimenting with various formats and examining what was available to his listeners on other stations, Geller decided to play only classical music—no all-talk, no news, no weather—just classical music. Thus, Geller was not covering controversial issues of local importance—and was in violation of the "fairness doctrine." The FCC tried to take away his license despite the fact that there were at least 30 other stations available to Geller's listeners, including an all-news station. After a legal battle of *10 years*, the court overturned the FCC's decision. In the interim, however, many stations hearing about Geller's plight conformed to what they believed were the FCC's standards for "public interest" broadcasting. *In such an environment, the diversity of the marketplace is lost to government control.*

Government content controls patronize the audience by assuming that the government knows what is best for the entire nation of viewers and listeners. Indeed, one of the unstated assumptions in these controls is that the five men and women who sit on the Federal Communications Commission are better judges of what people should see and hear about controversial issues than the broadcast audience itself. Since broadcasters are more responsive to audience surveys (which are a measure of audience demand) than any other group in our society, and because citizens make decisions regarding political issues based on information from a variety of sources, government content controls are unwarranted in a pluralistic and free society.

Despite the tendency by some in Congress to use the networks as whipping boys, government officials might better turn to the vast majority of broadcasters to examine the impact of these rules. Small local broadcasters are the most affected and the most fearful of government content regulations. They lack resources with which to challenge complaints. Even unjustified complaints must be handled delicately; so, to avoid legal entanglements, broadcasters often give in to the demands of pressure groups. After one painful experience with the fairness doctrine, or upon hearing of the experience of a fellow broadcaster, broadcasters have often adopted a policy of refusing to air anything controversial even if the station manager believed the program to be first-rate.

Under the "fairness doctrine," local stations often had trouble determining what a controversial issue was, how much time it should be given, and who in the community represented responsible "contrasting views." Even members of the FCC admitted that the doctrine was abused because of the arbitrary way its rules were applied. James McKinney, Chief of the Commission's Mass Media Bureau, described how a "fairness assessment" was made:

> We ... sit down with tape recordings, [and] video tapes of ... what has been broadcast on a specific station. We

compare that to newspapers [and] other public statements that are made in the community. We try to make a decision as to whether the issue is controversial, and whether it is of public importance in that community, which may be 2000 miles away [from our offices in Washington, D.C.]. . . . [W]hen it comes down to the final analysis, we take out stop watches and we start counting [the] seconds and minutes that are devoted to one issue compared to [the] seconds and minutes that are devoted to the other side of the issue.[12]

Commissioner Mimi Dawson wrote in frustration, "It is virtually impossible for a broadcaster to read the [FCC's recent fairness decision] and know what its responsibilities are under the fairness doctrine."[13] In many cases, broadcasters simply threw up their hands and avoided controversial issues so that they would not have to endure the endless red tape of an FCC hearing, a court battle over access to their station, or worse, the loss of their license.

These financial threats hung over each television and radio station in this country; many went to costly hearings at the FCC before they were resolved. Defending against a fairness complaint was a sobering experience and indicates just how difficult ensuring a "truth standard" in a "diverse system" can be.

Consider the struggle of Eugene Wilken, former general manager of KREM-TV in Spokane, Washington. Wilken recalled that a complaint arose immediately following KREM's one-time airing of a 60-second editorial endorsement of EXPO 74. Four people identifying themselves as representatives of an environmental group entered the station's offices and demanded air time to rebut the editorial. They wanted their version of diversity. Wilken asked for proof they represented some "responsible" group in the community. These "environmentalists" turned out to be a splinter group of eight neighbors who had broken off from the major environmental organization in the city. Wilken denied them access to the station's broadcast facility. They filed with the FCC. This seemingly minor confrontation snowballed into a major hearing during which KREM's staff was interviewed extensively by the FCC and KREM's files were searched. After $20,000 in legal fees, 480 hours of executive time, a delay in license renewal and four years of hearings and delays, KREM was exonerated. However, Wilken's career was ruined when he was fired for getting the station into the fairness quagmire.

It should, therefore, come as no surprise that many scholars who testified on the fairness doctrine before hearings of the Senate Commerce Committee in 1982 and 1984 believed that existing rules had a chilling effect on the discussion of issues by broadcasters. This testimony makes it all the more startling that, as we write, some members of Congress are seeking to *codify* the fairness doctrine into law despite a ruling by the U.S. Court of Appeals for the D.C. Circuit affirming the FCC's decision to repeal it.

Issue Advertising

The fairness doctrine also chilled issue advertising via the electronic media. The FCC has ruled that product advertising is not regulated, but the discussion of issues of public importance in ads was regulated until the doctrine was repealed. The logic: Allowing one side to be presented by an advertiser is unfair to the other side which might not have the resources of the advertiser. Therefore, in order to ensure diversity of opinion, issue ads triggered the fairness doctrine. Under this rule, Lee Iacocca is free to talk about the virtues of his American cars and their Japanese engines. But if Iacocca wanted to spend the 60 seconds his company bought arguing in favor of mandatory seat belt laws, he would effectively be precluded from doing so because stations or networks running the ads would face fairness complaints and be forced to defend their decision before the FCC, or would have to capitulate to requests for free time for those with contrasting views. In this case, that would mean giving time to Ralph Nader to explain why air bags are better than seat belts *and* to the Libertarian party to explain why the government has no right to order you to wear seat belts in your own car.

If the hypothetical example seems absurd, real ones seem insane. W.R. Grace and Company recently tried to air advertisements arguing against government waste and the federal deficit. The ads featured a courtroom set in the next century where a senior citizen is grilled by an adolescent prosecutor in front of a jury of children. "Didn't you know what your deficits would do" to our future? he is asked. The old witness, dressed in rags, withers under this attack and begs forgiveness. While some independent stations ran the ad, the networks found the ad too controversial. Finally, ABC relented and agreed to run the ad after 11:30 p.m.; then CBS said it would run the ad if references to a constitutional amendment to balance the budget were removed.

Mobil Oil offered to pay for the response time of those wishing to present contrasting views to their issue advertisements. The networks turned Mobil down because they would be put in the position of having to decide who should be chosen to respond to Mobil, a position fraught with litigious possibilities.

The Court has ruled that commercial speech is protected most of the time. Only when the government can prove that a restriction on commercial speech will advance an overriding government interest, can purely commercial speech be restricted.[14] However, if a political issue is discussed in the advertisement, or the ad provides information useful to the consumer's health, then the commercial speech is afforded First Amendment protection *in print*. Unfortunately, because issue advertising triggered the fairness doctrine, it faced a whole new set of regulations prior to the doctrine's repeal, and would again should the drive for codification succeed.

The Print Media

Content regulation also affects the print media. Those companies which own broadcast licenses—and most do—are targets for intimidation by the government or other parties. In a conversation with John Dean and H. R. Haldemann, then-President Richard Nixon advocated using the license renewal procedure at the FCC to intimidate the *Washington Post* through its television stations:

> *Nixon*: The main thing is the *Post* is going to have damnable, damnable problems out of this one. They have a television station—
>
> *Dean*: That's right, they do.
>
> *Nixon*: And they're going to have to get it renewed.

Of course, it was the *Post* that was doing the very investigating that would eventually lead to Nixon's downfall. Had Nixon succeeded in convincing others on his staff to use the FCC's power against the *Post*, American history might have been very different.

All of the press must be free from government intrusion if it is to provide the informing and perform the watchdog functions vital to the American democratic system. As the Founders well understood, all of our other basic liberties depend on sustaining freedom of expression. Governmental regulation was originally conceived as a means of regulating the use of AM radio frequencies. But government, with the support of some courts and Congress, has regulated every new technology of communication developed during the last 60 years—including cable television which is delivered by wire, not over the air. Nor have technological developments in the communications industry run their course.

One of the greatest dangers posed by government control over the content of electronic communications lies ahead. Technology is rapidly blurring the traditional line between print and broadcast journalism. With the advent of cable, videotex, and teletext, and the electronic delivery of news and other information, distinctions may soon be impossible to discern. *USA Today* and the *Wall Street Journal* already use satellites to beam their copy across the country to various printers. Many other newspapers are allowing their columns to be carried over teletext systems. The courts and the Congress face the difficult question of whether to extend print rights to the electronic media or to impose the controls applied to the electronic media to print.

Surely in a democracy such as ours, where freedom of expression is so highly valued, the burden of proof ought to be on those seeking to impose government restrictions, not on those who are providing an abundance of information. Perhaps that is why in the summer of 1984, in *FCC v. League of Women Voters*, the Supreme Court in two footnotes questioned the wisdom of retaining the *Red Lion* precedent. Said the Court:

> We note that the FCC, observing that "[i]f any substantial possibility exists that the [fairness doctrine] rules have impeded, rather than furthered, First Amendment objectives, repeal may be warranted on that ground alone," has tentatively concluded that the rules, by effectively chilling speech, do not serve the public interest, and has therefore proposed to repeal them.... As we recognized in *Red Lion*, however, were it to be shown by the Commission that the Fairness Doctrine "[has] the net effect of reducing rather than enhancing" speech, we would then be forced to reconsider the constitutional basis of our decision in that case.[15]

The Court went on to observe what anyone who has access to a television can see: The "scarcity of spectrum" rationale for the controls imposed by the government has been severely eroded. Given the explosion of electronic outlets such as cable, direct satellite broadcasts, and microwave signals, it is difficult to maintain that the electronic media should not be accorded parity with the print media. This among other reasons motivated the FCC to repeal the fairness doctrine on August 4, 1987. That decision was sustained by the U.S. Court of Appeals in 1989. But Congressman John Dingell, chairman of the House Committee on Energy and Commerce, and Senator Ernest Hollings, Rep. Dingell's counterpart in the Senate, have introduced legislation to reimpose the doctrine, overturning the two Court of Appeals decisions, *TRAC* and *Syracuse Peace Council*.

The Cross-Ownership Rules on Broadcasting and Newspapers

The attempt to achieve diversity through content controls is paralleled by the more recent attempts to achieve diversity through structural regulations. In 1975, the FCC imposed new rules which prohibited the cross-ownership of newspaper and broadcast entities in the same market.[16] To support this potential violation of the First Amendment, the FCC stated that it had the statutory authority to adopt such rules, and that the rules furthered its longstanding policy of promoting diversification of ownership and opinion. The Commission went on to note that, "The term public interest encompasses many factors including 'the widest possible dissemination of information from diverse and antagonistic sources.'"[17] Further, the Commission noted that although it was not empowered to enforce antitrust laws, it could properly take cognizance of antitrust violations in performing its public-interest licensing function.

During its investigation of the cross-ownership rules, the FCC took testimony from a vast array of sources. The findings of the Commission based on this research hardly supported the imposition of the rules. For example, the FCC said that commonly owned co-located newspaper-broadcast stations had a "long record of service" in the public interest. Many were pioneers in the broadcasting industry; they had established and continued traditions of service from the outset. Moreover, in its own study, the Commission found that, in terms of percentages of time devoted to several categories of local programming, co-located newspaper-owned television stations had displayed a statistically significant superiority over other television stations. Finally, the Commission made *no* findings that newspaper-broadcast combinations had not served the public interest, or that such combinations necessarily speak with one voice. No conclusions were drawn as to whether such combinations were harmful to competition, and the Commission expressly stated that it had found no pattern of specific abuses by existing cross-owners. Despite a record which, at best, was inconclusive with respect to any harm or potential harm cross-ownership may have posed, and, at worst, demonstrated the opposite, the Commission adopted the rules. It did this, said the Commission, to promote increased diversity. In short, the Commission believed the dream of diversity was more important than the reality of quality programming.

The Supreme Court upheld the FCC's authority as a "reasonable administrative response to changed circumstances in the broadcasting industry."[18] However, the Court pointed out that the competing goals of stability in the industry and preservation of competition were public-interest factors that the Commission could also take into account in fashioning the policy. The Court excluded "grandfathered" co-located entities from the rules but said the rules met constitutional scrutiny for new combinations because the rules allowed for waivers in hardship cases and the 1934 Act allowed regulation of licensees.

In 1987 and 1988, new evidence was found which indicated that the rules were not only unnecessary, but were counter-productive to their own goals. The argument that the rules are unnecessary is based on the same evidence used to demonstrate that scarcity is no longer applicable to the broadcast industry. (See the discussion above on the fairnesss doctrine.) In other words, the diversity of broadcast, cable, and other information outlets eliminates the need to control who owns which entities in a particular market. In its 1985 *Fairness Report* the FCC stated that these alternative electronic media had contributed significantly to the diversity of information available to the public, and had the potential of becoming substitute sources of information in the marketplace of ideas.

More important, however, is the argument that the rules impinge upon both the broadcaster's and the newspaper publisher's First Amendment rights. Although the regulation professes to be content neutral, restricting only ownership of broadcast facilities and not the content of their expression, it is precisely the nature of ownership that the Commission has asserted would advance or retard its own First Amendment objectives:

> The significance of ownership from the standpoint of "the widest possible dissemination of information" lies in the fact that ownership carries with it the power to select, to edit, and to choose the methods, manner, and emphasis of presentation, all of which are a critical aspect of the Commission's concern with the public interest.[19]

It necessarily follows that restrictions on ownership impinge on freedom of expression by determining who may speak, and who may not. Under the rules, newspaper publishers are denied the right to acquire a broadcast license in the same market solely because of their ownership of non-broadcast mass media facilities; broadcast licensees are forbidden to acquire a daily newspaper in the same market unless they relinquish their broadcast license.[20] The rules force the broadcaster and newspaper publisher to choose only one medium of expression to employ in a given market.

In addition to creating these First Amendment problems, the rules are also counterproductive in nature. Diversity of the electronic media has been achieved in spite of the rules through a proliferation of available allotments, by the development of new and competing technologies of information delivery systems, and by policies designed to encourage such new development, including *relaxation of the Commission's multiple ownership rules with regard to radio.* However, during the same period in which diversity in the electronic media was exploding, diversity in an important form of print media, the daily newspaper, was declining. Such a decline is a matter of grave concern generally, and has been recognized by a specific policy declaration of Congress.[21]

In 1910, there were 2,202 daily newspapers in this country, of which 2,140 were independent, that is, owned by someone who owned no other papers. At that time, 62 newspapers were group owned. By 1975, the year the cross-ownership rules were adopted, the total number of dailies had declined to 1,768, with only 650 independently owned. As of 1987, the total number of dailies had declined to 1,657, of which 1,223 (73.8%) were group owned.[22]

The decline in independent dailies is a result of suspended operations, acquisitions by newspaper chains, mergers with competing newspapers, and conversion to weekly formats. Not only has the number of daily newspapers declined, but so has their total combined circulation as a percentage of population. Finally, as the Commission has even noted, the number of competitive dailies has also declined. In 1965, 22 of the top 50 markets had competition between and among dailies; by 1986, that number had been cut in half. That same period also saw 53 closures and mergers; the only new daily newspaper started since 1965 that is still being published is the *Washington Times*. So much for diversity of news and information sources.

Faced with a number of failing newspapers that had attempted to remain viable through the use of joint operating agreements, Congress declared in 1970 that it was *in the public interest* to maintain "a newspaper press editorially and reportorially independent and competitive in all parts of the United States."[23] The "Newspaper Preservation Act" exempted newspaper joint operating agreements from antitrust laws, if, at the time of the arrangement, not more than one of the newspapers involved in the arrangement "was likely to remain or become a financially sound publication." From the statistics cited above, it may be concluded that the conditions which prompted Congress to act in 1970 have not been ameliorated, but have continued to grow worse in terms of diversity among print outlets.

The cross-ownership rules removed one significant method whereby a struggling daily newspaper might achieve greater economic stability, through affiliation with a co-located broadcast outlet.[24] Elimination of the rules would promote media diversity in the long run by permitting new and traditionally marginal newspaper operations to compete more effectively with the electronic media in general and grandfathered co-located newspaper-broadcast combinations in particular. Greater economies of scale through greater revenue bases, consolidation of office space, and consolidation of certain business and accounting functions would achieve economic stability without jeopardizing editorial integrity.

There is also considerable evidence that elimination of the rules would enhance program service. Co-located newspaper-television combinations have provided, to use the Commission's words, "statistically significant superiority" in a number of program particulars. They provide more local news and more local programming than do non-cross-owned stations.

When the FCC relaxed the rules governing joint ownership of AM and FM radio stations in the same market, it argued that the rules were no longer needed because of the diversity of voices available in the marketplace and because suspension of the rules would allow for significant cost savings in the operations of the radio stations. Said the Commission, "In a market with 50 media voices, it may be incorrect to assume that a 51st voice will necessarily enhance diversity more than an existing broadcaster who desires to operate an additional station in the same market."[25] Clearly, this observation applies with equal force to newspaper-broadcast operations.

Conclusion

Because freedom of expression is the foundation of all other rights, it is desirable to apply the full rights of the printed press to all other media of mass communication on the ground that the original regulations governing electronic outlets are anachronistic, counterproductive, and inimical to the ideals of our Founders.

The time has come to strike a new balance which will not only ensure greater freedom of expression for communication media but will at the same time provide authentic diversity among information providers. The elimination of outdated, constitutionally suspect, and damaging regulations can revitalize the free marketplace of ideas while providing better protection for the media's First Amendment rights.

III. The Misapplication of the Diversity Principle to Cable Television

The federal government has also sought to extend the diversity principle to the cable-television industry, with equally unsatisfactory results. A look at the history of cable regulation, including the Cable Communications Policy Act of 1984, confirms this gloomy assessment.

Cable-Television Regulation Prior to the Cable Act of 1984

In the late 1940s and early 1950s cable television, or Community Antenna Television (CATV), began to improve reception of over-the-air broadcast channels in small rural communities. These early systems generally operated by placing a large television antenna on a nearby hill and running cable to individual homes in the community. The systems were limited to retransmitting television signals from neighboring cities which otherwise could not be received without interference. During this period of cable's development, many systems functioned free of any form of regulatory control.

As cable television moved from retransmitting broadcast signals to providing a diverse mix of national programming, broadcasters (among others) sought regulations to control what they perceived to be harmful and monopolistic competition. Broadcasters feared that cable's ability to offer consumers alternative choices would lead to a division of audiences, which ultimately could cause a loss in advertising revenues for local stations. In 1958, broadcasters requested that the FCC regulate cable as a common carrier under Title II of the Communications Act of 1934. This request led to the first jurisdictional decision regarding cable television: The FCC found that cable fell outside the purview of the Communications Act.[1] Congressional attempts to regulate the cable industry by amending the Communications Act failed.

Bowing to pressure from broadcasters, the FCC determined in 1962 that applicants for common-carrier facilities proposing to serve the new cable industry must first prove that local broadcasters would not be financially harmed.[2] In two subsequent decisions,[3] the FCC extended its regulatory authority over all aspects of cable television under Section 2(a) and Section 307(b) of the Communications Act.

The Supreme Court in *United States v. Southwestern Cable Co.*[4] affirmed the FCC's jurisdiction over cable television. The Court recognized FCC authority to regulate cable television as "ancillary" to other regulatory powers over broadcasting granted in the Communications Act. Bolstered by the Court's holding in *Southwestern*, the Commission adopted "origination" rules which, among other things, provided that a cable operator with 3,500 or more subscribers could no longer retransmit any over-the-air broadcast signal unless it also offered a significant amount of cable-originated programming—non-broadcast—and maintained studios for local production.[5] In spite of the Commission's assertion that the rules were ancillary in purpose, they actually reflected a new perception of cable television from that of a mere conduit for delivering over-the-air broadcast signals to a facility for providing viewers with diverse program sources. Thus, in 1969 the Commission for the first time interjected the *diversity* concept into its regulation of cable television.

In 1971 in *United States v. Midwest Video Corp.* (*Midwest Video I*),[6] the Supreme Court sustained the Commission's expanded view of its statutory authority without abandoning the ancillary doctrine of *Southwestern*. *Midwest Video I* gave the FCC virtually total regulatory authority over cable television. As a consequence, in 1972 the Commission promulgated "access" rules which required cable operators to make certain channels available for public, educational, government, and leased-access use.[7] In addition, the cable operator had to provide facilities and production equipment for producing government and leased-access programming. Finally, under the Commission's rules, the cable operator was not allowed to choose who could use the channels, and was barred from exercising any editorial discretion over program content.

In *FCC v. Midwest Video Corp. (Midwest Video II)*,[8] the Supreme Court in 1979 struck down the Commission's access rules as exceeding the scope of authority outlined in *Southwestern* and *Midwest Video I*. The Commission argued that under *Midwest Video I* its access rules fell within its purview to encourage the maximum number of outlets for local expression, and to promote program diversity. The Commission—albeit unsuccessfully—based its authority to compel access to a cable operator's privately owned system squarely on the diversity principle.

Midwest Video II is significant because the Supreme Court limited the FCC's authority to regulate under the seemingly broad umbrella of the diversity principle. In addition, for the first time the Court indicated that a cable operator's First Amendment rights should not be dismissed out of hand. In a footnote, the Court acknowledged that the constitutional issues were not "frivolous" and observed that "the Commission's rules might violate the First Amendment rights of cable operators."[9] However, it did not decide the constitutional question; instead it struck down the access rules on statutory grounds.

In *Home Box Office, Inc. v. FCC*[10] (a case decided in 1977 two years prior to *Midwest Video II*), the United States Court of Appeals for the D.C. Circuit did address the constitutional question in a lengthy opinion involving the Commission's pay-cable regulations. The rules were intended to protect over-the-air broadcasters by preventing program suppliers from "migrating" from "free" television to pay-cable services. Finding the record insufficient to support the Commission's rulemaking process, the Court struck down the rules as failing the "ancillary to broadcast" standard of *Southwestern*. In addition, the Court addressed the constitutional question regarding the scope of permissible restrictions that could be placed on a cable speaker consistent with the First Amendment.

The Court began by rejecting the contention that cable's First Amendment rights were governed by *National Broadcasting Co. v. United States*[11] and *Red Lion Broadcasting Co. v. FCC*.[12] Both cases turned on the concept of "spectrum scarcity" as a rationale for government regulation. The Circuit Court in *Home Box Office* found, however, that spectrum scarcity did not exist in cable television. The Court observed that the number of available cable channels was sufficient to accommodate the number of persons seeking access to the cable system, and that future cable channel capacity would increase as technology developed. Moreover, the Court rejected the contention that cable television's alleged tendency to form a "natural economic monopoly" in the local community could serve as a basis for applying a more limited First Amendment protection than that afforded newspapers:

> [S]carcity which is the result solely of economic conditions is apparently insufficient to justify even limited government intrusion into the First Amendment rights of the conventional press and there is nothing in the record before us to suggest a constitutional distinction between cable television and newspapers on this point.[13]

Thus, cable was assured of more First Amendment protection over content than was the broadcast medium. However, its economic flank remained exposed to local control.

Regulating Under the Cable Act of 1984

From its humble beginnings, cable television experienced extensive and often oppressive regulation from local and state authorities. Even the FCC adopted various rules over time limiting the cable operator's freedom to program its own channels. In addition, because cable systems used the streets and public rights-of-way, local governments took an active, often aggressive role in regulating cable television. As Senator Barry Goldwater observed, there was a "patchwork of Federal, State, and local regulations and court decisions . . . . The result has been an unstable regulatory environment that has been bad for the cable industry, bad for the local and State franchising authorities, and bad for consumers."[14] Finally, in the first major amendment to the Communications Act in 50 years, Congress adopted the Cable Communications Policy Act of 1984.[15] While giving primary authority to the FCC, the Cable Act continued to permit local authorities to grant franchises and to fix the terms under which cable systems would operate.

The Cable Act tries to "assure that cable communications provide and are encouraged to provide the widest possible diversity of information sources and services to the public," and to "promote competition in cable communications and minimize unnecessary regulation that would impose an undue economic burden on cable systems."[16] However, it discounts these two goals by codifying local government authority to limit the number of cable systems, to assess franchise fees equal to 5 percent of a cable operator's gross income, and to encumber system capacity through mandated access.

Limiting the Number of Speakers: Single Franchises. The Cable Act permits a local government to award "1 or more franchises within its jurisdiction."[17] It also bars cable operators from providing service without first obtaining a franchise. In *Preferred Communications, Inc. v. City of Los Angeles*,[18] the only case since enactment of the Cable Act to come before the Supreme Court, a prospective cable operator challenged a city ordinance restricting the number of cable systems in the South Central District of Los Angeles to a single franchisee. The operator argued that the provision violated its First Amendment right to publish without government interference. The city argued that three factors brought cable TV within its regulatory authority: the "physical scarcity" of space on utility poles for hanging cable; the limited consumer demand—"economic scarcity"—for a second cable system serving Los Angeles; and the disruptive effect of construction on the public streets.

The United States District Court for the Central District of California dismissed the complaint, finding that the city's franchise rule did not violate the cable operator's First Amendment rights. However, the United States Court of Appeals for the Ninth Circuit reversed the lower court's decision. The Ninth Circuit Court declined to apply the broadcast standard to cable television, noting that each new medium of expression requires a different First Amendment standard and that "[d]espite the superficial similarity between broadcasting and cable television ... [t]he Supreme Court's determination to allow greater government intrusion into the affairs of broadcasters rests on the physical scarcity of radiowaves."[19] Physical and economic scarcity, according to the Circuit Court, do not justify the same First Amendment standard applicable to broadcasting.[20] Rejecting the broadcast standard set out in *Red Lion*, the Circuit Court expressed the view that cable television demonstrated sufficient editorial control to merit the same First Amendment standard applied to newspapers.

In 1986, the Supreme Court affirmed the Circuit Court's decision and remanded the case for further proceedings on the First Amendment question.[21] The Court noted that the First Amendment protects cable operators as well as broadcasters—notwithstanding the fact that by reason of spectrum scarcity broadcasters enjoy a limited right subject to government regulation.[22] Moreover, the Court recognized that a cable operator exercised editorial options analogous to those of a newspaper publisher or pamphleteer.[23] However, without a fully developed record, the Court affirmed the appellate court on narrower grounds.

But the United States Court of Appeals for the Eighth Circuit, focusing on the fact that the Supreme Court affirmed on narrower grounds, felt free to interpret *Preferred* as leaving the First Amendment question open. The lower court held that where a "natural monopoly" exists, cable might be distinguishable from newspapers and require more regulation than other media. In *Central Telecommunications, Inc. v. TCI Cablevision, Inc.*,[24] the Eighth Circuit ruled that the monopolistic characteristics of the Jefferson City cable market justified the city's offering an exclusive franchise. The only evidence cited for a natural monopoly was a study by the accounting firm of Touche Ross finding that "a direct house-to-house competition between two cable companies would not be financially feasible in Jefferson City . . . ."[25] Once the Court concluded that "there was economic capacity for only one [cable] speaker,"[26] it permitted the city to choose among competing applicants for the single franchise.

The Court moved from finding a natural monopoly to judging which of the two parties would advance the greatest First Amendment interests. In the Court's judgment, Central Telecommunications' proposed system "went further in advancing the First Amendment" than TCI Cablevision, somehow adding support for upholding the city's grant of an *exclusive* franchise:

> It is difficult for us to see how, on this record, TCI's position enhances First Amendment values. It is true that TCI has a First Amendment interest in remaining as a cable television "speaker," but Central has a similar interest. [G]iven the technology offered by the competing companies . . . it seems clear that Central's proposal went further in advancing the First Amendment . . . .[27]

The existence of a natural monopoly (if indeed it can be proved by a single study) still fails to provide a constitutional basis for government to choose the First Amendment speaker *it* believes will speak best or most efficiently. The Court's subjective selection of First Amendment speakers based on their proposed cable systems ignores First Amendment analysis. Let us suppose this Court found that Jefferson City could only support one newspaper; under its reasoning the government could choose that paper which it believed would provide the best news coverage.

The First Amendment constructs an absolute bar to any government body abridging the freedom of speech. The Supreme Court addressed and resolved the question of whether one speaker may be restricted in favor of another in *Buckley v. Valeo*:

> [T]he concept that government may restrict the speech of some elements of our society in order to enhance the relative voice of others is *wholly foreign* to the First Amendment, which was designed "to secure the widest possible dissemination of information from diverse and antagonistic sources."[28]

Although *Central* was primarily concerned with competition for cable television in Jefferson City, the Court's discussion regarding the First Amendment implications of single franchises represents a serious threat to free-speech rights.

Generally, when governmental regulations require a choice between two or more speakers, the First Amendment demands that courts weigh the validity of the asserted governmental interest against possible less restrictive alternatives of serving the same end. The Eighth Circuit failed to do either. The appropriate First Amendment standard for sole-franchise agreements remains that articulated by the Supreme Court in *Preferred*. That case rejects the broadcast theory of regulation embodied in *Red Lion*, and adopts the less restrictive newspaper model.

Imposing Special Taxation on Cable Speakers: Franchise Fees. The Cable Act also encourages abuse by authorizing payment of franchise fees based on a percentage of a cable system's gross revenues. The First Amendment does not bar cities from charging reasonable fees to help defray the costs of administering a cable franchise. However, it does bar any tax or charge on the constitutional right to speak. Since the Supreme Court recognized in *Preferred* that a cable operator's activities "plainly implicate First Amendment interests,"[29] the Cable Act's failure to restrict franchise fees to the city's legitimate administrative costs exceeds the constitutional limitation and violates the First Amendment. Singling out one speaker to raise revenue for city coffers cannot justify the substantial government interest required to sustain a First Amendment challenge. As the Supreme Court found in *Minneapolis Star & Tribune Co. v. Minnesota Commissioner of Revenue*,[30] a tax that singled out newspapers unconstitutionally "burden[ed] rights protected by the First Amendment."[31] The governmental interest in raising revenue was insufficient to justify the tax because "the State could raise the revenue by taxing businesses generally, avoiding the censorial threat implicit in a tax that singles out the press."[32]

The most recent case to address the constitutional implications of cable franchise fees is *Century Federal, Inc. v. City of Palo Alto*.[33] Relying on *Minneapolis Star*, the United States District Court for the Northern District of California found in 1988 that the city's franchise fee violated the First and Fourteenth Amendments to the Constitution. The Court noted that because other users of the city's public rights-of-way were not charged a fee or were charged at reduced rates, the franchise fee singled out the cable operator. The Court noted:

> This fact suggests that the goal of the regulation is not unrelated to suppression of expression . . . . A power to tax differentially, as opposed to a power to tax generally, gives government a powerful weapon against the taxpayer selected . . . . When the state singles out the press . . . the threat of burdensome taxes becomes acute. That threat can operate as effectively as a censor to check critical comment by the press, undercutting the basic assumption of our political system that the press will often serve as an important restraint on government . . . .[34]

But confusion reigned in 1988 when, in *Erie Telecommunications, Inc. v. City of Erie, Penn.*,[35] the United States Court of Appeals for the Third Circuit upheld a lower court's determinations that franchise fees were justified as a condition of a commercial enterprise's right of passage over public lands. While recognizing that a general tax on the right to speak would not be permissible, the lower court found that the city may charge a rental fee for use of public rights-of-way held in trust for the public.

The appellate court found it unnecessary to address the constitutional issues, holding that Erie Telecommunications, Inc. (ETI) had "agreed that the franchise agreement was 'valid, binding and of full force and effect,' and agreed to release the city from 'any and all claims . . . relating to . . . the Franchise' . . . ."[36] The Court observed that ETI had "knowingly, voluntarily, and intelligently relinquished any constitutional causes of action" when it entered into the franchise agreement with the city.[37]

The circular logic of the Third Circuit's rationale in *Erie* sets a dangerous precedent for cable-industry attempts to challenge franchise fees and access requirements. Stated simply, if the cable operator agrees to the terms of the franchise (which generally contains mutual releases and provisions for assessment of franchise fees) the cable operator will be barred from asserting future constitutional claims. However, if the cable operator refuses to agree to the city's demands, the city can deny the franchise and bar the cable operator from exercising its free-speech rights within the city. Remember that the Cable Act prohibits any cable operator from providing cable service without a franchise, and permits the city to award an exclusive franchise. Therefore, if the cable operator refuses to agree to the unconstitutional provisions of the franchise agreement, the operator will lose the right to operate as a cable speaker.

Moreover, the same conditions can result in forfeiture of channel capacity for public access, requirements to build television studios for city use, or mandated interconnection of municipal buildings with sophisticated two-way voice, video, and data networks. The Cable Act advocates the "widest possible diversity of information sources and services to the public,"[38] then allows local governments to reduce the cable operator's channel capacity by setting aside government-mandated access channels. Most cities use their power to grant an exclusive franchise to extract concessions from the cable operator—far more than a city could if the parties were in equal bargaining positions. Cities, of course, have no such extortionate power over newspaper publishers or broadcasters.

Government-Imposed Diversity: Mandated Access Channels. The Cable Act permits local governments to require that "channel capacity be designated for public, educational, or governmental use." Further, the Act prohibits cable operators from "exercis[ing] any editorial control over any public, educational, or governmental use of channel capacity" set aside for access programming.[39]

Congress desired that cable television, with its abundance of channels, offer the public "meaningful access" to the electronic media. It justified its action through the diversity principle. "They [access channels] provide groups and individuals who generally have not had access to the electronic media with the opportunity to become sources of information in the electronic marketplace of ideas." Moreover, "[a] requirement of reasonable third-party access to cable systems will mean a wide diversity of information sources for the public—the fundamental goal of the First Amendment ...."[40]

However, Congress failed to consider that access-channel requirements can clog a cable system's channel capacity and limit the *operator's* First Amendment right to provide a diverse program mix over its own system. Mandated access gives the city and other users a "free ride" on the local cable system. Worse yet, compelling cable operators to accept indiscriminately all speakers wishing to use mandated access channels interferes with editorial autonomy.

The fundamental protections afforded by the First Amendment serve a dual purpose. The First Amendment guards against government-ordered speech and, except under very narrowly defined conditions, prevents government from prohibiting the speech of others. The Cable Act violates both principles. It codifies federal and local government controls on the cable operator through mandated access channels, thereby diminishing the cable operator's editorial control by compelling it to carry all manner of messages.

Moreover, in the case of "government access" channels, the government itself coerces the cable operator to provide equipment, financial support, and channel capacity to deliver government speech. Clearly, the authors of the First Amendment never intended to precondition the exercise of free speech on the obligation that the speaker must also publish the views of government. As the Supreme Court observed in *Miami Herald Publishing Co. v. Tornillo*,[41] "[l]iberty of the press is in peril as soon as the government tries to compel what is to go into a newspaper."[42] The Court found that:

> The choice of material to go into a newspaper . . . and treatment of public issues . . . constitute the exercise of editorial control and judgment. It has yet to be demonstrated how governmental regulation of this crucial process can be exercised consistent with First Amendment guarantees of a free press . . . .[43]

The *Miami Herald* Court rejected arguments that "government has an obligation to ensure that a wide variety of views reach the public."[44] In fact, the Court found the opposite true:

> An enforceable right of access necessarily calls for some mechanism, either governmental or consensual. If it is governmental coercion, this at once brings about a confrontation with the express provision of the First Amendment and the judicial gloss on that Amendment developed over the years.[45]

Further, in *Midwest Video II*, decided prior to the Cable Act, the Supreme Court rejected similar attempts by the FCC to impose mandated-access channels to promote a diversity of viewpoints:

> [W]e reject the contention that the Commission's access rules will not significantly compromise the editorial discretion actually exercised by cable operators. At least in certain instances the access obligation will restrict expansion of other cable

services .... And even when not occasioning the displacement of alternative programming, compelling cable operators indiscriminately to accept access programming will interfere with the determinations regarding the total service offering to be extended to subscribers.[46]

In short, the First Amendment simply does not support a right of access—to newspapers or to cable television. The First Amendment precludes Congress from compelling public and government access to the media (although this prohibition has been eroded in the case of radio and broadcast television). Furthermore, even if one accepts the dubious "spectrum scarcity" rationale for affording broadcasters lesser First Amendment rights, no such condition exists in cable television. As the United States Court of Appeals for the D.C. Circuit in *Home Box Office*, and more recently in *Quincy Cable TV, Inc. v. FCC*,[47] observed, "Unlike ordinary broadcast television, which transmits the video image over airwaves capable of bearing only a limited number of signals, cable reaches the home over coaxial cable with the technological capacity to carry 200 or more channels."[48] Clearly the First Amendment bars government involvement in speech via mandated access or exclusive franchising.

Conclusion

Franchise fees, mandatory access channels, and limited franchises—codified in the Cable Communications Policy Act of 1984—are an abrogation of cable speakers' First Amendment rights. Franchise fees require cable operators to pay a fee tantamount to a tax on the right to speak. Mandatory access channels permit cities, under the guise of promoting diversity of information sources, to wrest editorial control from cable operators. Government-mandated "access channels" coerce speech by abrogating a cable operator's control over the composition of its programming. Finally, limited franchising vests power in the government to choose which First Amendment speakers it will allow—and which it will deny—to provide information to the public.

Freedom of expression protected by the First Amendment facilitates public discussion. Regulating information flow through franchise fees, mandatory access channels, and exclusive franchises to advance information diversity frustrates the First Amendment values such regulation attempts to promote. Moreover, this involvement falls outside permissible boundaries of legitimate regulation, even in a marketplace limited by scarce resources. The First Amendment bars government involvement in speech; it clearly implies that measures taken to promote diversity are permissible only when they encourage a multiplicity of outlets. Measures imposed to force a particular media outlet to represent a diversity of viewpoints offend the First Amendment. It would be much more consistent with the intent of the Founders to allow several cable systems to operate in the same area, and to end mandatory access and franchise fees. Cable subscribers would then be free to encourage the diversity *they* desired.

IV. The Misapplication of the Diversity Principle to the Telecommunications Industry

The misuse of the diversity principle reached its zenith in 1982 in *United States v. American Telephone & Telegraph Co.*[1] In that case, the United States District Court for the District of Columbia entered a consent decree on antitrust grounds prohibiting AT&T and the divested Bell Operating Companies (BOCs) from entering the electronic publishing industry. The Court reasoned that because the BOCs controlled the transmission network that electronic publishers needed, the BOCs would act anticompetitively by excluding competing publishers and thereby frustrate the First Amendment goal of diversity. Thus, the Court used the diversity principle to harmonize the First Amendment with antitrust laws to promote competition in the information market; in the process, it imposed content restrictions on the newly divested BOCs.

In its unprecedented reading of the First Amendment, the District Court also speculated that the BOCs could gain monopoly control over news and information in the United States. However, an analysis of First Amendment case law reveals that restricting one speaker to enhance another falls outside the permissible realm of governance.

The Court's application of the diversity principle to the electronic publishing industry not only violates the principles inherent in the First Amendment, but actually prevents new information services from entering the market.[2] During the first triennial review of the consent decree, the District Court for the District of Columbia dismissed any contention that information restrictions infringed upon the BOCs' First Amendment rights.[3]

This chapter will survey the development of telephone regulation regarding content-based restrictions imposed to promote First Amendment values, and will examine the diversity principle in the context of today's information services industry.

*The Diversity Principle—
A Legitimate Means of Serving a Compelling Government Interest?*

Justice Holmes forewarned that the "ultimate good desired is better reached by free trade in ideas"[4] rather than by government decree. The "marketplace of ideas" presupposes the diversity principle: "the widest possible dissemination of information from diverse and antagonistic sources."[5]

Justice Holmes' concept of a "free trade in ideas" cuts both ways. On the one hand are those who argue that a "self-operating marketplace of ideas long ceased to exist . . . [and that a] realistic view of the First Amendment requires recognition that a right of expression is somewhat thin if it can be exercised only at the sufferance of the managers of mass communications."[6] On the other hand are those adhering to the First Amendment's clear language that "Congress shall make no law . . . abridging freedom of speech . . . ." The latter view, in its simplistic form, holds that "truth" and diversity need no help from Congress. In fact, when government involves itself in ordering truth, speech invariably suffers and is often limited.

These two diametrically opposed theories—"hands off" versus affirmative governmental regulation—conflict each time technology opens another avenue of communication. Courts have given steady recognition to the idea that each new medium carries with it unique characteristics justifying variations in the First Amendment standards applied to it. How courts have responded to these justifications turns largely on how they view the nature of the medium.

When government imposes content-based restrictions on any new medium, the applicable First Amendment test requires government to show that the regulation represents a *precisely drawn* means of serving a *"compelling" government interest*.[7] In content-based restrictions, First Amendment values define the government interest as promoting diversity in information sources available to the American public. Generally, courts adhere to the absolute language in the First Amendment barring government intrusion into content. The government interest fails to reach a "compelling" level absent some extraordinary condition. In the early days of broadcasting, "spectrum scarcity" was thought to be such a condition.

As discussed in Chapter 2, the Supreme Court in *Red Lion* dismissed the concept that every broadcaster possesses an unabridgeable First Amendment right.[8] The Court reasoned that in a limited spectrum, where government must involve itself to maintain order, those receiving a broadcast license do not enjoy First Amendment rights on par with other avenues of speech. In *Red Lion* the Court found diversity a compelling government interest by reason of spectrum scarcity, and found the Personal Attack Rule narrowly tailored to serve that end. This ruling has come under considerable attack and the Court has indicated a willingness to review the issue.

In *Miami Herald*, decided just four years after *Red Lion*, the Supreme Court reached the exact opposite conclusion and struck down a state statute designed to promote diversity in the newspaper industry. The Court refused to broaden the spectrum-scarcity touchstone developed in *Red Lion* to include "economic scarcity." In fact, the Court did not mention *Red Lion* at all in its *Miami Herald* decision. Instead, the Supreme Court rejected the plaintiff's argument that because economic conditions made entry into newspaper markets difficult, the government could impose a limited right of access to the press. Thus, the fact that more persons want to enter the newspaper market than economic conditions permit does not create a "compelling" government interest justifying regulation to maintain diversity.

Similarly, content-based restrictions founded on "physical scarcity" do not satisfy the test. In *Preferred Communications, Inc. v. City of Los Angeles*[9] (discussed in Chapter 3) the Supreme Court rejected the City of Los Angeles' "physical scarcity" argument. Because of the limited physical space available for stringing cable and the potential disruptive effect of construction on city rights-of-way, the city had intended to maintain content-based regulations to promote diversity consistent with the First Amendment.

Moreover, in 1985 the Circuit Court of Appeals for the District of Columbia directly confronted and rejected the contention that the monopoly nature of cable television afforded a lesser First Amendment right justifying intrusive government regulation. In *Quincy Cable TV, Inc. v. FCC*,[10] the Court addressed the "spectrum-scarcity" versus the "economic-constraints-on-competition" debate, and weighed in favoring First Amendment rights. Citing *Miami Herald*, the Court "categorically rejected the suggestion that purely economic constraints on the number of voices available in a given community justify otherwise unwarranted intrusions into First Amendment rights . . . ."

Only content-based restrictions based on spectrum scarcity remain sufficiently compelling to withstand a First Amendment challenge. However, even the Supreme Court in *Red Lion* realized that a regulation which reduced, rather than actually promoted, diversity would warrant a different result. In a case where diversity was reduced, the means would not be sufficiently tailored to serve the legitimate end—diversity. This then would constitute a violation of the First Amendment proscription on government involvement in free-speech rights.

Common Carriers: The Breakup of AT&T

Congress and the courts did not consider the relevance of the First Amendment when they developed the legal framework for the telephone industry. The 19th century law developed to regulate canals and railroads—common carriers transporting goods—provided telephone technology with its legal theory.[11] Applying railroad law to the early telegraphy and telephone cases resulted in over 100 years of common-carrier regulation lacking in any consideration of potential First Amendment issues. Likewise, until Judge Harold Greene entered the *"Modification of Final Judgment"* (*MFJ*), the diversity principle never applied to the telephone industry.

Prior to the *MFJ* decision, AT&T, operating as a regulated monopoly, built a sophisticated nationwide telecommunications network. The *MFJ* restructured AT&T, requiring divestiture of its telecommunications holdings in the private intercity telephone service markets and equipment manufacturing industry. The *MFJ* effected a complete restructuring of the telecommunications market. Competition rather than regulated monopoly would drive the new structure. AT&T and the divested Bell Operating Companies would now compete in a dynamic industry that no longer confined itself to providing basic telephone service to customers. The new telecommunications industry included an array of electronic services that could provide a limitless number of avenues for communication. The various services, dubbed "electronic publishing," crossed all boundaries: television, public forum, newspapers, audio services, data, text, and two-way interactive services that would permit users to access large libraries of information. The restructuring of the telecommunications industry, and the advent of these new services, required a reexamination of the traditional common-carrier mode of regulating. The traditional passive carrier, forced to compete in a dynamic communications market, began asserting its right as a speaker.

Recognizing First Amendment Implications in Common-Carrier Decisions. In *United States v. American Telephone and Telegraph Co.*,[12] the United States District Court for the District of Columbia, for the first time in a common-carrier case, considered the First Amendment relevant in rendering a decision. The case arose in 1974 when the Department of Justice (DOJ) filed suit against AT&T, Western Electric, and the Bell Telephone Labs. The DOJ charged the defendants with illegal use of monopoly power to impede competition in the telecommunications equipment and private intercity telephone service markets in violation of the antitrust laws. The government sought to break up the AT&T monopoly by requiring divestiture of the Bell Operating Companies (BOCs) and Western Electric.

The DOJ and AT&T reached a settlement on the modification of a 1956 consent decree[13] in January 1982. The District Court for the District of Columbia made certain modifications and entered final judgment approving the consent decree on August 11, 1982.[14] The Supreme Court granted *certiorari*, and without opinion summarily affirmed the District Court's order. The required divestiture took place on January 1, 1984 and effectively restructured the telecommunications industry.

The District Court imposed post-divestiture restrictions on the BOCs on the assumption that they possessed both the incentive and the opportunity to use their monopoly power to act anticompetitively. The Court conceded the anticompetititve effect of its restrictions, but concluded that the already competitive information market did not need the BOCs.[15]

The District Court reasoned that because information-service providers required the use of the telecommunications network controlled by the BOCs, a potential risk existed that the BOCs would (1) cross-subsidize their own information services to the disadvantage of their competitors; and (2) possess the incentive to discriminate against competitors by restricting access to the local networks they controlled. The Court maintained that if the BOCs were excluded from information services, they would be motivated instead to design a telecommunications network that could "accommodate the maximum number of information service providers."[16] Thus, the Court believed that restricting the BOCs from becoming electronic publishers would both enhance competition and be consistent with the principles of antitrust laws. Moreover, the Court imposed a virtually impossible standard for removal of the information restrictions. The standard provides that "[t]he restrictions imposed upon the separated BOCs . . . shall be removed upon a showing . . . that there is no substantial possibility that [a BOC] could use its monopoly power to impede competition in the market it seeks to enter."[17]

After recognizing the First Amendment implications of its decision, the Court concluded that permitting the divested companies to engage in electronic publishing would pose a substantial threat to other electronic publishers. Therefore, the Court would prohibit the BOCs from entering the market in the interest of diversity. The Court applied content restrictions on AT&T and the divested BOCs according to what might be termed a "competitive scarcity" theory. By relying on the long line of broadcast precedent in which the government interest in regulating content outweighed a speaker's First Amendment rights by reason of spectrum scarcity, the Court equated competitive scarcity to spectrum scarcity and found that the information restrictions furthered the public interest.[18]

The MFJ Triennial Review. In approving the terms of the *MFJ*, the District Court for the District of Columbia retained authority to enforce the provisions of the decree by providing for a triennial review. In accordance with the triennial review process, on February 2, 1987 the DOJ filed its *Report and Recommendations of the United States Concerning the Line of Business Restrictions Imposed on the Bell Operating Companies by the Modification of Final Judgment*[19] ("DOJ Report"). This was accompanied by a document entitled *The Geodesic Network: 1987 Report on Competition in the Telephone Industry*, prepared by Dr. Peter Huber ("Huber Report"). The DOJ advocated elimination of the information-service prohibition entirely. It found that FCC regulations—specifically Computer Inquiry III[20] and joint and common cost-allocation rulemaking—were sufficient to prevent a reoccurrence of the abuses which led to the antitrust suit in 1974.

The DOJ based its recommendation on an extensive study conducted by Dr. Huber. The Huber Report found that since the AT&T divestiture, the structure of the communications industry had evolved from a "hierarchical pyramid" toward a dispersed, homogeneous "geodesic" network. In a geodesic network, control rests with the individual network users in an array of small switching systems. The geodesic network limits the ability of any one organization to exercise monopolistic control over competitors. Thus, the telecommunications industry is becoming decentralized, less concentrated and more competitive, warranting removal of the line-of-business restrictions. Moreover, the Huber

Report found it impossible for a BOC to leverage its single regional network to impede competition in an information-services industry which operated on a national and international scale.

Release of the DOJ Report launched an armada of response briefs from intervenors including BOC competitors and potential competitors, trade associations, and state regulators. On March 13, 1987, the FCC observed that restricting the BOCs' entry into the electronic publishing business actually diminished the public interest.[21] The FCC asserted that less information resulted from the information restriction, rather than more.

On September 10, 1987, the District Court issued its opinion retaining the content restriction imposed by the 1982 decision.[22] The Court rejected the DOJ's assertion that sufficient competition now existed to warrant removal of the information restrictions. The Court based its conclusion on a competitive analysis of the local market in which the BOCs controlled the transmission network—rather than the national market identified in the Huber Report—finding information-service providers remained regionally dependent on the BOCs' local exchange facilities. In addition, the Court rejected DOJ recommendations to transfer oversight of the *MFJ* to the FCC. The Court criticized FCC regulations as ineffective in preventing anticompetitive abuses.

On March 7, 1988, the Court released a further opinion. The Court permitted the BOCs to offer a system of gateways for the use of the information-service industry, but continued to prohibit the BOCs from providing information they owned or controlled.[23] The Court rejected arguments that the domestic information market needed the BOCs to keep up with foreign competition. In addition, the Court saw no advantage to the domestic information industry if the content restrictions were lifted from the BOCs. It concluded that the BOCs lacked the necessary experience in the information industry to make a difference. Moreover, it added that the BOCs possessed no particular expertise in the electronic publishing business and that they were "not needed in these aspects of American business." The BOCs appealed the triennial review and subsequent decisions to the Circuit Court of Appeals for the District of Columbia.

Substituting Competitive Scarcity for Spectrum Scarcity

In the *MFJ* decision and the subsequent triennial review, the District Court found that the BOCs, as common carriers, required a different First Amendment treatment than that applied to traditional publishers.[24]

However, the District Court failed to recognize that a single entity can be both a common carrier in one instance and not in another. Thus, in those services not offered on a common-carrier basis, the BOCs should enjoy the same First Amendment protections as other corporations and members of the public.

The District Court asserted a twofold interest. First, under antitrust laws the Court sought to remedy AT&T's past anticompetitive conduct by ordering divestiture of its local phone companies. And second, the Court intended to promote diversity by preventing concentration of ownership and control in the information-services industry from emerging in the newly divested BOCs. To promote diversity, the Court restricted the BOCs' ability to participate in the information-services industry. The Court speculated that, absent the BOCs, competition would flourish. The Court thus equated spectrum scarcity with competitive scarcity, and imposed a complete ban on the divested BOCs' right to speak and publish over their own (or anyone else's) facilities.

The Court used antitrust laws to prevent the newly divested BOCs from entering the information-services market. Antitrust laws serve a legitimate governmental interest, but in some instances courts must fashion antitrust remedies that affect the First Amendment rights of speakers. The antitrust laws generally place structural barriers on the anticompetitive practice at issue in a particular case. If the practice involves speech then the court must structure the remedy narrowly to serve both the interests of the antitrust laws and those of the Constitution.[25] A "narrowly drawn" remedy represents one in which the illegal conduct can reasonably be eliminated by fashioning an appropriate restraint on future conduct. However, placing a total ban on the BOCs' ability to engage in speech to promote the speech of potential competitors violates the Supreme Court's holdings in First Amendment cases; therefore, the ban cannot be accepted as reasonable.[26] Moreover, in no case does the Supreme Court permit a complete ban on one speaker to promote diversity.

Thus, the fact that the BOCs control a portion of the transmission paths used by their competitors cannot justify depriving the BOCs of their First Amendment rights to use their own facilities. The potential scarcity of electronic publishers is not compelling enough to prevent a willing speaker from publishing. While the courts may fashion antitrust remedies to curtail anticompetitive activities, they must balance competing First Amendment interests. The District Court failed to account for both interests in barring the BOCs from speaking.

Furthermore, the District Court failed to consider the potential prior-restraint implications of its order.[27] The *MFJ* restriction prevents the BOCs from transmitting their information over the telephone network, and thus denies information to that segment of the public wanting BOC-generated material.[28]

In addition, content-based restrictions to promote diversity by reason of competitive scarcity necessarily require government to choose one speaker over another. Under this model, the voice which is most efficient or effective must be suppressed. But suppressing speech by reason of its efficiency or effectiveness does an injustice to the First Amendment. Directly regulating content because of the effectiveness of the speech, or indirectly regulating to promote classes of speakers, surely subverts Oliver Wendell Holmes' dream of an open marketplace of ideas. Such regulation is even more onerous given the lack of any evidence of anticompetitive behavior by the BOCs in information services.

Conclusion

Clearly, government involvement in promoting diversity in the name of the First Amendment can undercut the very goals it seeks to advance. Such involvement falls outside permissible boundaries of legitimate regulation. Regulations developed in the early 20th century no longer accord with the reality of the burgeoning telecommunications networks of today. Scarcity no longer exists. Telecommunications networks provide a multitude of competing channels for individual expression. The United States District Court for the District of Columbia, accepting the changing nature of telecommunications, redefined the spectrum-scarcity rationale for regulating speech as scarcity in competition, or "competitive scarcity." This approach represents an expansion of government power to regulate the content of speech.

In a society where cable, optical fiber, and satellites abound, concerns about scarcity of any kind seem irrelevant. Since 1969, for example, when the Supreme Court decided *Red Lion*, the number of radio and television stations has dramatically increased. In addition, the personal computer alone has given millions of individuals a host of new ways to communicate. We now speak of desk-top publishing, electronic publishing, information services, information-retrieval systems, on-line libraries, electronic mail, voice mail, and networking. Even the idea of the public billboard has changed to incorporate sophisticated electronic message boards. Public policies founded on principles developed in the 1920s are no longer flexible enough to keep pace with this rapidly changing technological environment. Because of the rapid pace set by technology, policy tends to inhibit rather than promote freedom.

The *MFJ* decision provides a stark example of the District Court for the District of Columbia's reaction to the changing telecommunications industry. The Court actually developed a rule which violates the First Amendment in an effort to preserve it. This approach could lead to more and more restrictions until the words "Congress shall make no law . . . abridging the freedom of speech" retain little or no meaning. As Justice Bradley remarked in 1886: "It may be that it is the obnoxious thing in the mildest and least repulsive form; but illegitimate and unconstitutional practices get their first footing in that way, namely by silent approaches and slight deviations from legal modes of procedure."[29] The solution to this dilemma is two-fold: the development of an informed understanding of the diversity principle and its appropriate applications; and a renewed adherence to the clear language of the First Amendment which prohibits government from making any law repressing speech.

V. Conclusion

In the foregoing sections, we have examined the misapplication of the diversity principle. Four major cases emerged, each involving modern media.

First, until its repeal, the so-called fairness doctrine chilled the speech of broadcasters and issue advertisers, at the same time imposing costly administrative and legal burdens. While the promulgation of the doctrine was undoubtedly well intentioned—a corrective on a rule prohibiting editorializing by broadcasters—it nonetheless provided a weapon by which special-interest groups and the federal government could harass and intimidate broadcasters.

Agreeing with this assessment, the FCC found the doctrine to be counterproductive, in violation of the public interest, and unconstitutional. The FCC's repeal of the doctrine was upheld by the Circuit Court of Appeals for the District of Columbia. But the issue is not closed. Legislation was introduced in Congress to overturn the FCC's decision by codifying the doctrine into federal law. While a majority in both houses supports codification, enough senators may oppose it to sustain a presidential veto as they did in 1987 and 1988.

The second major problem has also been prolonged by mischievous legislative action. At the close of the 1987 congressional session, a hidden provision was included in the omnibus, thousand-page continuing resolution. It forbade the FCC from re-examining its broadcast-newspaper cross-ownership rules. Several groups including the American Newspaper Publishers Association, the National Association of Broadcasters, and the Freedom of Expression Foundation filed petitions requesting that the FCC inquire into the rules. These requests were based on research which revealed that (1) the rules had been adopted in 1975 without cause, that is, without any finding that cross-owned stations or newspapers served the public less well than non-cross-owned entities; (2) independent newspapers are declining in number and need co-located broadcast stations for support; (3) cross-owned broadcast stations had a better record of public service than non-cross-owned stations; (4) the rules favored cross-owned stations that were "grandfathered" over newer stations in the same market that had to compete with them; and (5) the ownership restrictions violated the First Amendment's protection of access, free speech, and press.

These rules remain in effect today despite the fact that they are counterproductive. Worse, the FCC is precluded by law from even convening an inquiry into the merits of these charges.

The third problem arises from the misapplication of the diversity principle to the cable industry. Despite the fact that most cable systems offer a multitude of channels, information, and viewpoints, they have consistently been subjected to structural and content controls. For example, the federal government has applied the fairness doctrine to original cable programming. And until the *Quincy* decision, cable owners were required to carry all broadcast stations within 50 miles even if these stations duplicated programming among themselves.

Many hoped that the Cable Communications Policy Act of 1984 would remedy this problem. But the Act codified certain local franchising powers which has led to numerous court cases attempting to determine cable's First Amendment standing. In the meantime, local governments have required cable companies to provide "citizen access" and "educational" channels, to transmit meetings of local governments, and to pay excessive franchise fees. They have also prevented new cable companies from entering a market where one already exists, thereby denying consumers a choice among cable companies, and limiting prospective cable companies' ability to speak in a given market.

These practices have been challenged in the courts on First Amendment grounds. The only case which the Supreme Court has heard affirmed cable's standing as a First Amendment provider with rights roughly akin to those of a newspaper publisher. Many more cable cases will have to be decided before the status of cable with regard to structural and content restrictions is understood.

The fourth problem concerns restrictions placed on telecommunications companies forbidding them from becoming electronic publishers of information. These restrictions certainly do not increase diversity. They clearly endanger America's ability to develop new technologies which can compete on the world market. The telephone companies, given their capital and research capabilities, are the most likely to keep America competitive in the international information age. And yet, they are precluded from developing the very technologies in which they have demonstrated expertise.

Worse is the restriction on First Amendment rights. Again we have a case of consumers being denied access to information and major providers being denied access to citizens. Telephone companies as information providers can greatly expand the marketplace of ideas. Yet, based on the unproven assumption that they would engage in anticompetitive behavior, the Court has prevented their entry into the marketplace. Because free speech is so highly valued in our system, we believe the burden of proof should fall on those who would restrict the free flow of information, rather than on information providers. In short, those who wish to preclude telephone companies from providing information in *any* market must first prove that those companies have acted in a way that would close down part of the marketplace. Until the burden is assumed, telephone companies should be given access to the information marketplace.

Our discussion of these problems suggests certain obvious solutions:

(1) Sustain the repeal of the fairness doctrine;
(2) Repeal the newspaper-broadcast cross-ownership rules;
(3) Protect cable's First Amendment rights by ending mandated access channels, franchise fees, and exclusive franchising; and
(4) Allow telephone companies to enter the information marketplace.

What may be less obvious are the principles this study has generated, a set of principles which will render the diversity principle more coherent, more supportive of technological development, and much more consistent with First Amendment goals. We conclude this study by articulating these principles.

Principle 1. **The marketplace of ideas is more important than the regulations that govern it.** In this century, there has been a tendency to become so entranced with making the market fair and equitable that rules have been adopted which actually prevent ideas from being expressed. The notion that an open and robust exchange of thought leads to the truth can be traced to Aristotle. In a free arena, ideas are given an equal opportunity to compete, but no one assumes that they are equal in merit. The weaker lose to the stronger; the false are defeated by the true. While ideas do battle, the citizen as spectator or participant becomes increasingly educated and performs his or her civic duty with more knowledge. That was the Founders' dream for a properly functioning democracy.

Thus, barring a national emergency or a "compelling" government interest, the free marketplace of ideas should never be compromised. Applying this principle to the cases we have examined refocuses our critical lens and helps us to understand why counterproductive rules, even the most well intentioned, must be struck down if they inhibit freedom of expression. We believe ample evidence exists to make such a case against the fairness doctrine, the cross-ownership rules, federal and local restrictions on cable, and the rules preventing telephone companies from becoming electronic publishers.

***Principle 2.* Diversity must be understood in the context of the entire marketplace of ideas.** Each shop in a shopping mall does not offer the same products. If it did, there would be no need for more than one shop. The important question: Does the marketplace *as a whole* meet the consumer's needs? Does it provide a diverse selection?

It is no different in the marketplace of ideas. If government requires each shop—each newspaper, each television station, each cable company—to provide the same ideas, then many ideas, undoubtedly the most radical, will be shunted aside. Homogeneity will reign and progress will come to a halt.

Instead, the marketplace of ideas must be viewed as a mix of shops providing all sorts of information. A shop may wish to specialize in what it does best: *National Review* editorializes; Cable News Network provides continuous news; DIALOG provides information services. Each provides consumers with a higher quality product than would be the case if they were forced to provide government-mandated information. Thus, content rules should not be applied to the communications media as long as the marketplace as a whole is providing diverse information to its citizens.

We have demonstrated throughout this study that the marketplace is flooded with diverse ideas. The likelihood is not that the citizen will be deprived of ideas; it is rather that he or she will be overwhelmed by them. That fact leads us to the next principle.

***Principle 3.* Scarcity is an outmoded and dangerous rationale for content regulations.** In the first two chapters of this study, we demonstrated that scarcity of broadcast outlets no longer exists, and that even if it did, it would be a dangerous tool for policymaking. There are over 10,000 radio stations and 1,300 television stations in this country. Ninety-five percent of all homes receive five or more television stations; two-thirds of those homes have access to cable. Magazines, newspapers, and computer data overload our brains. Arguments that scarcity exists sink very quickly in such a sea of information.

More important, in 1789 when the First Amendment was written and in 1791 when it was adopted, the Founders did not consider the scarcity of access to newspapers—neither economic access nor editorial access—to be a valid reason to restrict the eight dailies that existed at the time. Judge Bork's comment on this principle bears repeating:

> [I]t is unclear why [scarcity] justifies content regulation of broadcasting in a way that would be intolerable if applied to the editorial process of the print media. All economic goods are scarce, not least the newsprint, ink, delivery trucks, computers, and other resources that go into the production and dissemination of print journalism. Not everyone who wishes to publish a newspaper, or even a pamphlet, may do so. Since scarcity is a universal fact, it can hardly explain regulation in one context and not another.

Two years before Judge Bork's decision in *TRAC*, which the Supreme Court refused to reconsider, it said in *FCC v. League of Women Voters*:

> [I]n light of the substantial increase in the number and types of information sources, we believe that the artificial mechanism of interjecting the government into the affirmative role of overseeing the content of speech is unnecessary to vindicate the interest of the public in obtaining access to the marketplace of ideas.

Taken together, these opinions reveal that the scarcity rationale was bad policy in the first instance and is certainly outmoded now. To use it to justify the imposition of government regulation is disingenuous and damaging to the marketplace of ideas.

***Principle 4.* The government should not favor one speaker over another.** While equal opportunity to the marketplace must be safeguarded, the government must not enter the arena and give advantage to one participant over another. For example, under the fairness doctrine, broadcast editorials are limited; newspaper editorials are not. Under Judge Greene's application of the diversity principle, telephone companies cannot enter the information-services business while newspapers can. Under the Cable Communications Policy Act, local governments can select one cable company and reject others. And the cross-ownership rules have given a competitive advantage to "grandfathered" co-located entities over new outlets. Both economic and information distortions take place under such a system. It is incompatible with our democratic values and certainly inconsistent with the spirit of the First Amendment.

Principle 5. **Where the First Amendment is involved, antitrust regulations should be applied only where anticompetitive practices have been found to exist.** Even these regulations should be applied narrowly on a case-by-case basis.

This principle derives from the fact that First Amendment freedoms are precious and provide the foundation for all other rights. If we deprive a speaker of these sacred rights, then we had best have a very good reason for doing so. Speech that threatens the national security, presents a clear and present danger, or is without redeeming social value and violates narrowly drawn legislation, forfeits its protection. But in the contexts we have examined, speech which *may* have the potential of being anticompetitive has been denied First Amendment protection. Most notably this is the case with the telephone companies' request to enter the information-services business. In our opinion, the fact that the Bell Operating Companies control a portion of the transmission paths used by their competitors cannot justify depriving the BOCs of their First Amendment right to publish information.

Principle 6. **Government fear of the persuasive power of new technology should not be used as a rationale for regulations.** Throughout recorded history, rulers have attempted to place restrictions on new technology for fear it would threaten their power or enhance the power of their subjects. The Germanic princes of Gutenberg's time placed restrictions on his new press as soon as he demonstrated how it worked by printing a Bible. When the new press arrived in England in 1476, it was met with suspicion. Within a few years it was censored and licensed.

The plight of the electronic media in America has been no different. Every new medium of communication invented in this century has been regulated by the federal government. While some restrictions can be justified for the sake of efficiency or a clear signal, many others have allowed government agencies, notably the FCC, to oversee editorial policy and technological development.

Justice William Brennan explained the government's motive in a commencement address at Brandeis University in 1986:

> Rulers always have and always will find it dangerous to their security to permit people to think, believe, talk, write, assemble, and particularly to criticize the government as they please. But the language of the First Amendment indicates that the Founders weighed the risks involved in such freedoms and deliberately chose to stake this government's security and life upon preserving the liberty to discuss public affairs intact and untouchable by government.

This study, its recommendations, and the principles it has generated are aimed at restoring the First Amendment environment of which the Founders dreamed. It is not an easy task to convert government policy, court cases, and congressional actions into a coherent, fair, and consistent program that advances the First Amendment interests of all concerned. But that is just what we have attempted to do here. While much work must still be done in terms of briefs, legislative relief, and further research, we hope we have provided a framework from which a strengthened commitment to the free marketplace of ideas can grow.

Notes

Chapter One

[1] 376 U.S. 254 (1964).

[2] 326 U.S. 1 (1945).

[3] 395 U.S. 367 (1969). *See also National Broadcasting Co. v. United States*, 319 U.S. 190 (1943).

[4] With the rapid development of electronic media, the Supreme Court has said that with some signal from Congress or the FCC this decision should be re-examined because the scarcity rationale may no longer apply. *See FCC v. League of Women Voters*, 468 U.S. 364, 376 n.11, 378 n.12 (1984).

[5] 418 U.S. 241 (1974).

[6] In *FCC v. League of Women Voters*, the Supreme Court said:

> We note that the FCC . . . has tentatively concluded that the rules, by effectively chilling speech, do not serve the public interest, and has therefore proposed to repeal them. . . . As we recognized in *Red Lion* . . . were it to be shown by the Commission that the fairness doctrine "[has] the net effect of reducing rather than enhancing" speech, we would then be forced to reconsider the constitutional basis of our decision . . . . *Id.* at 378 n.12.

Since that decision, the FCC repealed the doctrine, and was sustained in *Syracuse Peace Council v. FCC*, 2 FCC Rcd. 5043, 5047 (1987), aff'd on nonconstitutional grounds, 867 F.2d 654, 669 (D.C. Cir. 1989) by the U.S. Court of Appeals.

56 THE DIVERSITY PRINCIPLE

[7] 20 F.C.C.2d 201, 220 (1969).

[8] *Id.* at 221-22.

[9] *See* 53 Rad. Reg. 2d (P&F) 1309 (1983). While reserving authority to impose content rules on teletext, the FCC chose in this case not to do so. This action was challenged by the Telecommunication Research Action Center (TRAC) in *TRAC v. FCC*, 801 F.2d 501 (D.C. Cir. 1986), *cert. denied*, 482 U.S. 919 (1987). On September 19, 1986, in an opinion written by Judge Robert Bork and supported by Judge Scalia, the U.S. Court of Appeals ruled that the FCC had the discretion under the law to apply or not apply the rules as it saw fit. In short, the Court said the fairness doctrine had not been codified.

[10] *See Final Report and Order in Docket No. 18509* (Section 214 Certificates), 21 F.C.C.2d 307, *modified*, 22 F.C.C.2d 746 (1970), *aff'd sub nom. General Tele. Co. of Southwest v. United States*, 449 F.2d 846 (5th Cir. 1971).

[11] *See United States v. American Tele. and Tele. Co.*, 552 F. Supp. 131 (D.D.C. 1982), *aff'd sub nom. Maryland v. United States*, 460 U.S. 1001 (1983). *See also United States v. Western Elec. Co.*, 1988-1 Trade Cas. (CCH) ¶67918 (D.D.C. Mar. 7, 1988).

[12] 567 F.2d 9 (D.C. Cir.), *cert. denied*, 434 U.S. 829 (1977).

[13] *CableSpeech: The Case for First Amendment Protection*, (New York: Harcourt, Brace and Jovanovich, 1983), p. xv.

[14] (1978) §§12-22, at 697.

[15] 418 U.S. 241 (1974).

[16] 108 S. Ct. 2138 (1988).

[17] *United States v. Western Elec. Co.*, 673 F. Supp. 525 (D.D.C.), *appeal docketed*, No. 87-5388 and consolidated cases (D.C. Cir. Nov. 30, 1987).

[18] Department of Justice, *Newsrelease*, February 2, 1987, p. 4.

[19] Judge Greene permitted the BOCs to offer such services as voice mail and enhanced transmission of electronic databases because newspapers have no interest in providing such services. But Judge Greene re-emphasized that the BOCs were prohibited from generating content for information services.

[20] 424 U.S. 1 (1976).

Chapter Two

[1] 418 U.S. 241, 258 (1974). When President Reagan vetoed the Fairness in Broadcasting Act of 1987 on June 20, 1987, he referred to this decision in his rationale.

[2] 395 U.S. 367 (1969).

[3] *National Broadcasting Co. v. United States*, 319 U.S. 190, 215-16 (1943).

[4] *Editorializing by Broadcast Licensees*, 13 F.C.C. 1246 (1949).

NOTES   57

5. In *Telecommunication Research and Action Center v. FCC*, 801 F.2d 501 (D.C. Cir. 1986), *cert. denied*, 482 U.S. 919 (1987), Judge Bork, in which Judge Scalia joined, ignored the legislative history of the 1959 attempt to codify the fairness doctrine and said the amendment only gave the FCC primary jurisdiction if it chose to apply the doctrine. Since the Supreme Court did not grant *certiorari* in this case, the Court's ruling stands.

6. Senator William Proxmire (D-Wis.), who sponsored the law, tried to get it repealed after he saw its effect.

7. The equal time rule is actually the "equal opportunities" provision of Section 315 of the Communications Act of 1934 as amended, 47 U.S.C. §315(a). A broadcast licensee who gives air time to any legally qualified candidate must provide "equal opportunities" to all other legally qualified candidates for that same office. The access rule states that any station's license may be revoked "for willful or repeated failure to allow reasonable access to the use of a broadcasting station by a legally qualified candidate for Federal elective office on behalf of his candidacy." The fairness doctrine is not part of the 1934 Act, but a rule derived from an interpretation of the "public interest" standard. It deals with issues, not candidates. It requires that a licensee must devote a reasonable amount of time to the discussion of important issues in the locale of the station, and that coverage of such issues must be "balanced" or "fair." Contrasting viewpoints by responsible elements in the locale must be aired.

8. *See TRAC*, 801 F.2d at 508.

9. *Id.* at 508 n.4.

10. *CBS v. Democratic Nat'l Comm.*, 412 U.S. 94, 161 (1973) (Douglas, J. concurring).

11. Between 1980 and 1986, only 20 violations of the fairness doctrine were found and only 132 other cases went to hearing. Thousands of complaints were dismissed as frivolous or unworthy of consideration. *See Hearings on Freedom of Expression Act before the Commerce Committee*, 98th Cong., 2nd Ses. (1984).

12. *Fairness Report*, 102 F.C.C.2d 143, 191 (1985).

13. *Syracuse Peace Council v. Television Station WTVH*, 99 F.C.C.2d 1389, 1420 (1984) (Comm. Dawson dissenting).

14. *See* Craig R. Smith and M. Joel Bolstein, *All Speech Is Created Equal* (Washington, D.C.: Freedom of Expression Foundation, 1986); *see also Board of Trustees of the State Univ. of New York v. Fox*, 109 S.Ct. 3028 (1989).

15. 468 U.S. 364, 378 n.12 (1984).

16. Amendment of Sections 73.35, 73.240 and 73.636 of the Commission Rules Relating to Multiple Ownership of Standard, FM and Television Broadcast Stations, 22 F.C.C.2d 306 (1970)(First Report and Order). The text of the Multiple Ownership Policy reads in part:

"(c) No license for an AM, FM, or TV broadcast station shall be granted to any party (including all parties under common control) if such party directly or

58 THE DIVERSITY PRINCIPLE

    indirectly owns, operates, or controls a daily newspaper and the grant of such license will result in:
   (1) The predicted or measured 2 mV/m contour for an AM station . . . encompassing the entire community in which such newspaper is published; or
   (2) The predicted or measured 1 mV/m contour for an FM station . . . encompassing the entire community in which such newspaper is published; or
   (3) The Grade A contour for a TV station . . . encompassing the entire community in which such newspaper is published."

[17] The quotation by the FCC is from *Associated Press v. United States*, 326 U.S. 1, 20 (1945).

[18] *FCC v. National Citizens Comm. for Broadcasting*, 436 U.S. 775 (1978).

[19] Amendment of Sections 73.35, 73.240 and 73.636 of the Commission Rules Relating to Multiple Ownership of Standard, FM and Television Stations, 50 F.C.C.2d 1046 (1975)(Second Report and Order).

[20] It is well established that the government may not condition the receipt of a public benefit on the relinquishment of a constitutional right, especially the right to freedom of expression. *See Perry v. Sinderman*, 408 U.S. 593, 597 (1972); *Sherbert v. Verner*, 374 U.S. 398, 404 (1963); *Shapiro v. Thompson*, 394 U.S. 618 (1968).

[21] *See Newspaper Preservation Act of 1970*, 15 U.S.C. §1801-1804.

[22] *See Editor and Publisher Yearbook* (1986).

[23] *See Newspaper Preservation Act, supra* note 21.

[24] The *Newspaper Preservation Act* makes clear that economies of joint operation can be achieved without sacrificing editorial and reportorial independence.

[25] See Amendment of Section 73.3555 [formerly Sections 73.35, 73.240, and 73.636] of the Commission's Rules Relating to Multiple Ownership of AM, FM and Television Broadcast Stations, 100 F.C.C.2d 17 (1984).

Chapter Three

[1] *Frontier Broadcasting Co. v. Collier*, 24 F.C.C. 251, 256 (1958). In *Inquiry into the Impact of Community Antenna Systems, TV Translators, TV "Satellite" Stations, and TV "Repeaters" on the Orderly Development of Television Broadcasting*, 26 F.C.C. 403 (1959) the Commission continued to assert that it lacked jurisdiction over cable and reaffirmed its decision in *Frontier* that cable television fell outside the regulatory structure of the Communications Act of 1934. *Id.* at 427-28. In addition, the Commission determined that it would not consider the potential impact on local broadcasters when granting a license to a common carrier proposing to service the new cable industry. If the FCC were to assert jurisdiction it would have to come from Congress. *Id.* at 427-30.

[2] 32 F.C.C. 459 (1962), *aff'd*, 321 F.2d 359 (D.C. Cir. 1963), *cert. denied*, 375 U.S. 951 (1963).

[3] *Amendment of Subpart L, Part 11, To Adopt Rules and Regulations to Govern the Grant of Authorization in the Business Radio Service for Microwave Stations to Relay Television Signals for Community Antenna Systems*, 38 F.C.C. 683 (1965), *aff'd sub nom. Black Hills Video Corp. v. FCC*, 399 F.2d 65 (8th Cir. 1968) (initially imposing regulation of those cable systems receiving distant television signals via microwave transmission). *Amendment of Subpart L, Part 91, To Adopt Rules and Regulations to Govern the Grant of Authorization in the Business Radio Service for Microwave Stations to Relay Television Signals to Community Antenna Systems*, 2 F.C.C.2d 725, *aff'd sum nom. Black Hills Video Corp. v. FCC*, 399 F.2d 65 (8th Cir. 1968) (finding authority to regulate cable in the Communications Act itself).

[4] 392 U.S. 157 (1968).

[5] *See First Report and Order in Docket No. 18397*, 20 F.C.C. 2d 201 (1969), *rev'd sub nom. Midwest Video Corp. v. United States*, 441 F.2d 1322 (8th Cir. 1971), *rev'd*, 406 U.S. 649 (1972).

[6] 406 U.S. 649 (1972).

[7] *Cable TV Capacity and Access Requirements, Report and Order in Docket No. 20508*, 59 F.C.C.2d 294 (1976). The Commission first began requiring public, educational, and government (PEG) channels by its Order in 1972. *Cable Television Report and Order*, 36 F.C.C.2d 143, *on recon.*, 36 F.C.C.2d 326 (1972), *aff'd sub nom. ACLU v. FCC*, 523 F.2d 1344 (D.C. Cir. 1975).

[8] 440 U.S. 689 (1979).

[9] *Id.* at 709 n.19.

[10] 567 F.2d 9 (D.C. Cir.), *cert. denied*, 434 U.S. 829 (1977).

[11] 319 U.S. 190 (1943).

[12] 395 U.S. 367 (1969).

[13] *Id.* at 46 (citing *Miami Herald Publishing Co. v. Tornillo*, 418 U.S. 241, 247-56 (1974)).

[14] Cong. Rec. H10,435 (Oct. 1, 1984).

[15] Cable Communications Policy Act of 1984, Pub. L. No. 98-549, 98 Stat. 2779 (codified at 47 U.S.C. §§521-559 (Supp. III 1985)).

[16] *Id.* at §521(4),(6).

[17] 47 U.S.C. 541(a)(1).

[18] 754 F.2d 1396, 1403 (9th Cir. 1985), *aff'd on narrower grounds*, 476 U.S. 488 (1986).

[19] *Id.*

[20] *Id.* at 1404-05; *see also Quincy Cable TV, Inc. v. FCC*, 768 F.2d 1434, 1449-50 (D.C. Cir. 1985), *cert. denied sub nom.*, *National Ass'n of Broadcasters v. Quincy Cable TV, Inc.*, 476 U.S. 1169 (1986). The D.C. Circuit recognized that the "scarcity rationale" ha[d] no place in evaluating government regulation of cable television." *Id.* at 1449 (footnote omitted). The Court noted that "technological advances may have rendered the 'scarcity rationale' obsolete even for broadcasters." *Id.* at 1449 n.32.

[21] *Id.* at 496.

[22] *Id.* at 494-95; *see also Quincy*, 768 F.2d at 1447-48. In *Quincy*, the Circuit Court disallowed the economic scarcity rationale for affording cable television a lesser First Amendment standard. *Id.* at 1450. "[T]he Supreme Court has categorically rejected the suggestion that purely economic constraints on the number of voices available in a given community justify otherwise unwarranted intrusions into First Amendment rights." *Id.* In addition, the Court rejected the physical scarcity rationale. *Id.* at 1448-49.

[23] *Preferred*, 476 U.S. at 494; *see also Group W. Cable, Inc. v. City of Santa Cruz*, 669 F. Supp. 954 (N.D. Ca. 1987) ("[T]he starting point for the Court's analysis is that unless cable television differs in some material respect from the print media, the First Amendment standards that apply to newspapers apply with equal force to cable." *Id.* at 961. The District Court rejected the "physical scarcity" rationale for limiting pole access to a single cable system. *Id.* at 960-61.); *Century Fed., Inc. v. City of Palo Alto*, 648 F. Supp. 1465, 1470 (N.D. Cal. 1986) ("We recognize that 'differences in the characteristics of new media justify differences in the First Amendment standards applied to them.' Application of a lesser standard of protection, however, is an exception to the rule that must be justified by a particular difference." *Id.* "The threshold issue . . . is whether the First Amendment allows the government the same wide latitude in regulating the CTV industry as it allows in the broadcast medium or whether the degree of protection should be closer to that enjoyed by the traditional media, such as newspapers." *Id.*) (citations ommitted) (footnote omitted), *cert. dismissed*, 108 S. Ct. 1002 (1988).

[24] 800 F.2d 711 (1986).

[25] *Id.* at 717 n.6.

[26] *Id.* at 717.

[27] *Id.*

[28] 424 U.S. 1, 48-49 (1976) (emphasis added).

[29] *City of Los Angeles v. Preferred Communications, Inc.*, 476 U.S. 488, 494 (1986).

[30] 460 U.S. 575 (1983).

[31] *Id.* at 582.

[32] *Id.* at 586.

[33] *Century Federal*, No. C-85-2168, slip op. (N.D. Cal. Oct. 12, 1988).

[34] *Id.* at 23 (quoting *Minneapolis Star*, 460 U.S. at 585).

[35] 853 F.2d 1084 (3rd Cir. 1988).

[36] *Id.* at 1085-86.

[37] *Id.* at 1101.

[38] 47 U.S.C. 521.

[39] 47 U.S.C. 531(e).

[40] H.R. Rep. No. 98-934, 98th Cong., 2nd Ses., *reprinted in* 1984 U.S. Code Cong. & Admin. News 4655, 4667.

[41] 418 U.S. 241 (1974).

[42] *Id.* at 258 n.24.

[43] *Id.* at 258.

[44] *Id.* at 248.

[45] *Id.* at 254.

[46] *Midwest Video II*, 440 U.S. 689, 707-08 n.17 (1979).

[47] 768 F.2d 1434 (D.C. Cir. 1985), *cert. denied sub nom.*, *National Ass'n of Broadcasters v. Quincy Cable TV, Inc.*, 476 U.S. 1169 (1986).

[48] *Id.* at 1448.

Chapter Four

[1] 552 F. Supp. 131 (D.D.C. 1982), *aff'd sub nom. Maryland v. United States*, 460 U.S. 1001 (1983) (This case is commonly known as the Modified Final Judgment or "MFJ") [hereinafter *MFJ*].

[2] *See Report and Recommendations of the United States Concerning the Line of Business Restrictions Imposed on the Bell Operating Companies by the Modification of Final Judgment*, (filed Feb. 2, 1987), *United States v. Western Elec. Co.*, 673 F. Supp. 525, 104 (D.D.C. 1987) (noting that competition had flourished since the divestiture, the Department of Justice advocated elimination of the information services prohibitions on the BOCs in their entirety.) [hereinafter DOJ Report].

[3] *United States v. Western Elec. Co.*, 673 F. Supp. 525, 586 n.273 (D.D.C.), *appeal docketed*, No. 87-5388 and consolidated cases (D.C. Cir. Nov. 30, 1987).

[4] *Abrams v. United States*, 250 U.S. 616, 630 (1919) (Holmes, J. dissenting).

[5] *Associated Press v. United States*, 326 U.S. 1, 20 (1945).

[6] Barron, "Access to the Press—A New First Amendment Right," 80 Harv. L. Rev. 1641, 1666-78 (1967); *See also* Bollinger, *Freedom of the Press and Public Access*, 75 Mich. L. Rev. 1 (1976). Bollinger fails to distinguish among the various forms of media outlets (*e.g.* newspapers, television, radio, etc.) arguing that by their very

similarity government regulation is justified in the broadcast media, when counterbalanced by an unrestrained print media. Bollinger considers this the "best of two worlds." *Id.* at 27, 36. Bollinger's theory rests on the premise that Congress should maintain a partial regulatory structure for the sake of fostering two distinct First Amendment values, "access in a highly concentrated press and minimal government intervention." *Id.* at 36.

[7] *Consolidated Edison Co. v. Pub. Serv. Comm'n*, 447 U.S. 530, 540 (1980).

[8] *Red Lion Broadcasting Co. v. FCC*, 395 U.S. 367, 390 (1969).

[9] *Preferred Communications, Inc. v. City of Los Angeles*, 754 F.2d 1396, 1402 (1984) *aff'd* 476 U.S. 488 (1986).

[10] 768 F.2d 1434 (D.C. Cir. 1985), *cert. denied sub nom.*, *Nat'l Ass'n of Broadcasters v. Quincy Cable TV, Inc.*, 476 U.S. 1169 (1986).

[11] The Court concluded that the power to regulate this new industry rested in the commerce clause of the Constitution. U.S. Const. art. I, sec. 8, cl. 3. *See Pensacola Tele. Co. V. Western Union Tele. Co.*, 96 U.S. 1, 8-9 (1878). For a lengthy description of the legislative history of the Interstate Commerce Act of 1887 and its incorporation into Title II of the Communications Act of 1934, see *ABC v. FCC*, 643 F.2d 818, 820-22 (D.C. Cir. 1980). Had the courts treated the telephone as an extension of the newspaper (printed word) rather than the railroad (a transportation system for words) an entirely different legal structure might exist.

[12] 552 F. Supp. 131 (1982), *aff'd sub nom. Maryland v. United States*, 460 U.S. 1001 (1983).

[13] *Id.* at 131. In 1956 AT&T and the DOJ settled by consent decree similar charges involving violations of the Sherman Antitrust Act. 15 U.S.C. Sec. 2. *See United States v. Western Elec. Co.*, 1956 Trade Cas. (CCH) ¶68,246 (D.N.J. 1956). The 1956 decree precluded AT&T and its local phone companies from offering any services other than common-carrier communications, and confined Western Electric's equipment manufacturing to that used by the Bell System. In addition, the decree required the defendants to license patents held by the Bell System to all applicants on payment of royalties. *See* 552 F. Supp. at 178-79.

[14] The 1982 Decree required:
- Vacation of the 1956 Decree restricting AT&T to only providing common-carrier services;
- Divestiture of the 22 local Bell telephone companies (which then became the basis of the seven newly created Regional Bell Operating Companies—"RBOCs" or "BOCs");
- Guarantee of equal access to the BOCs' local telephone networks; and
- Restricting the BOCs from engaging in (1) information services; (2) interexchange services; and (3) the manufacture of telecommunications products.

[15] 552 F. Supp. at 189 ("The Operating Companies would simply be additional competitors in a market that is already quite competitive."). Moreover, the Court acknowledged that if it permitted the BOCs to enter competitive markets they would "be faced with the most potent conceivable competitor: AT&T itself." *Id.* at 187.

[16] *Id.* at 189.

[17] *United States v. Western Elec. Co.*, 673 F. Supp. 525, 532 (D.D.C. 1987), *appeal docketed*, No. 87-5388 and consolidated cases (D.C. Cir. Nov. 30, 1987).

[18] *MFJ*, 552 F. Supp. at 184.

[19] *Western Elec.*, 673 F. Supp. at 528 n.1.

[20] 104 F.C.C.2d 958 (1986), *modified*, 2 FCC Rcd 3035 (1987) Computer Inquiry III established safeguards against BOC monopolization by requiring implementation of Comparably Efficient Interconnection ("CEI") and Open Network Architecture ("ONA").

[21] *Comments of the FCC as Amicus Curiae on the Report and Recommendations of the United States Concerning the Line of Business Restrictions Imposed on the Bell Operating Companies by the Modification of Final Judgment*, at 7, *United States v. Western Elec. Co.*, 673 F. Supp. 525 (D.D.C. 1987) (No. 82-0192). [hereinafter *FCC Brief*].

[22] *Western Elec.*, 673 F. Supp. at 529.

[23] *United States v. Western Elec. Co.*, 1988-1 Trade Cas. (CCH) ¶ 67,918, 67,620 (D.D.C. March 7, 1988). The District Court allowed the BOCs to provide a "help" function and directions regarding how to locate and select information-service providers; "White Pages" electronic directories to the extent they included a listing of telephone subscribers with addresses and telephone numbers; electronic mail; and voice storage and retrieval services. *See Western Elec.*, 673 F. Supp. at 594-96.

[24] *Western Elec.*, 673 F. Supp. at 586 n.273.

[25] As a general proposition, the Supreme Court has not acknowledged any inconsistency or tension between the First Amendment and antitrust laws. *Associated Press v. United States*, 326 U.S. 1, 19-20 (1945); *Lorain Journal Co. v. United States*, 342 U.S. 143, 155-56 (1951). However, First Amendment considerations do influence how antitrust laws are applied in a case. *See Homefinders of Am., Inc. v. Providence Journal Co.*, 621 F.2d 441, 444 (1st Cir. 1980); *Levitch v. Columbia Broadcasting System, Inc.*, 495 F. Supp. 649, 660-62 (S.D.N.Y. 1980).

[26] *See Buckley v. Valeo*, 424 U.S. 1, 48-49 (1976) ("[T]he concept that government may restrict the speech of some elements of our society in order to enhance the relative voice of others is wholly foreign to the First Amendment, which was designed 'to secure the widest possible dissemination of information from diverse and antagonistic sources' ") (quoting *New York Times Co. v. Sullivan*, 376 U.S. 254, 266 (1964)); *see also Pacific Gas and Elec. Co. v. Pub. Util. Comm'n*, 475 U.S. 1, 20 (1986); *First Nat'l Bank of Boston v. Bellotti*, 435 U.S. 765, 790-91 (1978).

[27] The existence of the waiver process does not change the nature of the restraint. The BOCs still must seek prior clearance before speaking. "[U]nder the decree itself, [the information] restriction may be removed only if the Regional Companies are able to make a certain showing, again mandated by the decree, one that they have not made and could not make at this time." *Western Elec.*, 673 F. Supp. at 586 n.273.

64 THE DIVERSITY PRINCIPLE

[28] The First Amendment's proscription against abridging freedom of speech correlatively protects the rights of persons to receive ideas and information. "It is now well established that the Constitution protects the right to receive information and ideas." *Kleindienst v. Mandel*, 408 U.S. 753, 762-63 (1972) (quoting *Stanley v. Georgia*, 394 U.S. 557, 564 (1969)); *see Martin v. City of Struthers*, 319 U.S. 141, 143 (1943) ("this freedom embraces the right to distribute literature . . . and necessarily protects the right to receive it."); *see also Lamont v. Postmaster General*, 301 U.S. 301, 305 (1965) (finding the addressee's unfettered right to receive the mails paramount to asserted governmental interest); *Thomas v. Colins*, 323 U.S. 516, 534 (1945) (sustaining Texas workers' right to meet, discuss, and be informed of impending election for collective bargaining agent). "This right to receive information and ideas, regardless of their social worth, see [*Winters v. New York*,] 333 U.S. 507, 510 (1948), is fundamental to our free society." *Stanley*, 394 U.S. at 564.

The Supreme Court in *Red Lion Broadcasting Co. v. FCC*, 395 U.S. 367 (1969) extended the right to receive information to include listeners and viewers. "It is the right of the public to receive suitable access to social, political, esthetic, moral, and other ideas and experiences which is crucial here. That right may not be constitutionally abridged either by Congress or by the FCC." *Id.* at 390.

[29] *Boyd v. United States*, 116 U.S. 616, 635 (1886).

The Editor

Craig R. Smith has served as president of the Freedom of Expression Foundation since its inception in 1982. He is also a professor of communication at California State University at Long Beach where he directs the Center for First Amendment Studies. Dr. Smith received his Ph.D. from Pennsylvania State University in 1969 and began a teaching career that has taken him to San Diego State University, the University of Virginia, and the University of Alabama in Birmingham where he chaired the communication arts division. He has also spent a good deal of time in the political world including positions as Director of Senate Services for the Republican Conference of the U.S. Senate (1979), campaign manager for the re-election of Senator Bob Packwood (1980), and Deputy Director of the National Republican Senatorial Committee (1981-82). In addition, he has served as a consultant to CBS News for convention, election night, and inaugural coverage since 1968.

This volume is one of many books and articles that Dr. Smith has written or edited. His publications include *Partisan Politics and Freedom of Expression* (University of South Carolina Press, 1989); *Defender of the Union: An Oratorical Biography of Daniel Webster* (Greenwood/Praeger Press, 1989); and *Orientations to Speech Criticism* (Science Research Associates, 1982).

The Media Institute

The Media Institute is a nonprofit, tax-exempt research foundation supported by a wide range of foundations, corporations, associations, and individuals. The Institute publishes studies analyzing media coverage of major public-policy issues, and sponsors a host of programs related to the new technologies, the First Amendment, and other communications policy issues. To support the work of the Institute, or for further information, please contact Patrick D. Maines, President, The Media Institute, 3017 M Street, N.W., Washington, D.C. 20007.

Media Policy Series. Richard T. Kaplar, General Editor
Production: David P. Taggart

DATE DUE